THE Hillsong WORSHIP COLLECTION

ISBN 978-1-4584-0650-7

HAL•LEONARD® CORPORATION
7777 W. BLUEMOUND RD. P.O. BOX 13819 MILWAUKEE, WI 53213

Visit Hal Leonard Online at
www.halleonard.com

AT THE CROSS

Words and Music by REUBEN MORGAN
and DARLENE ZSCHECH

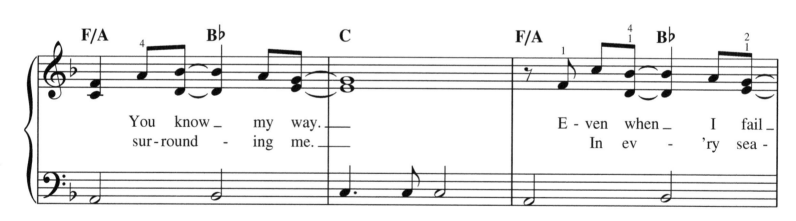

3

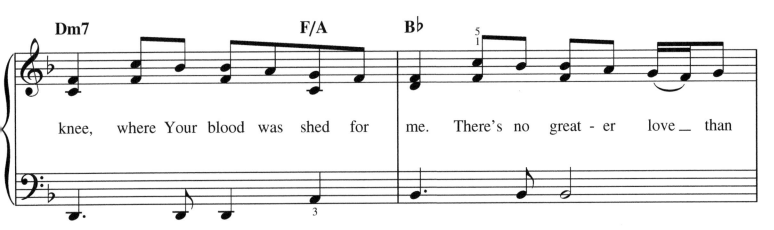

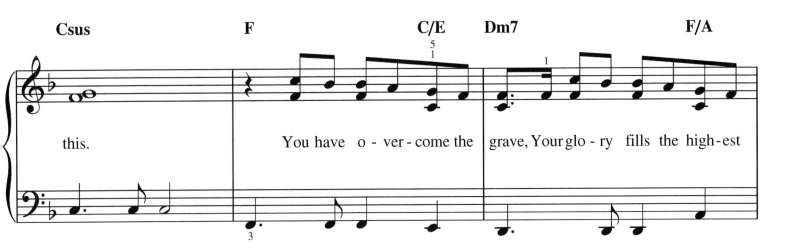

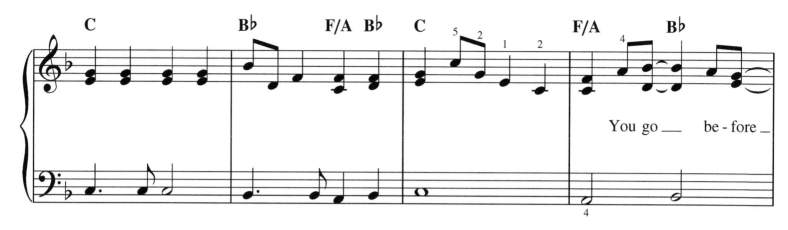

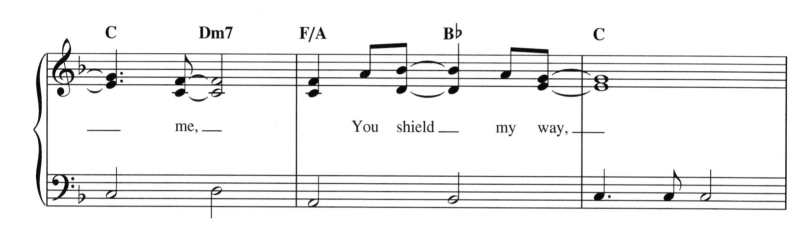

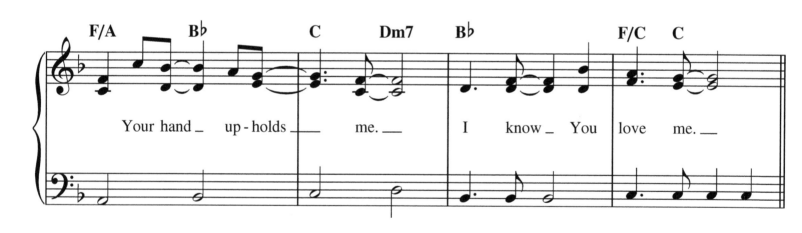

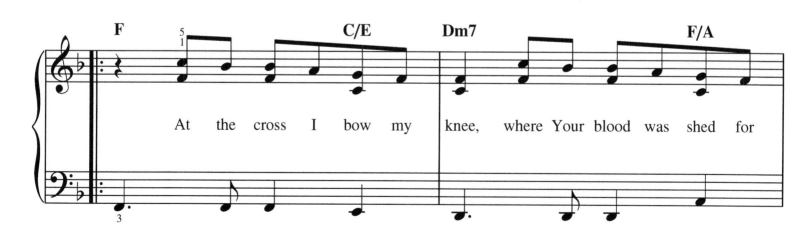

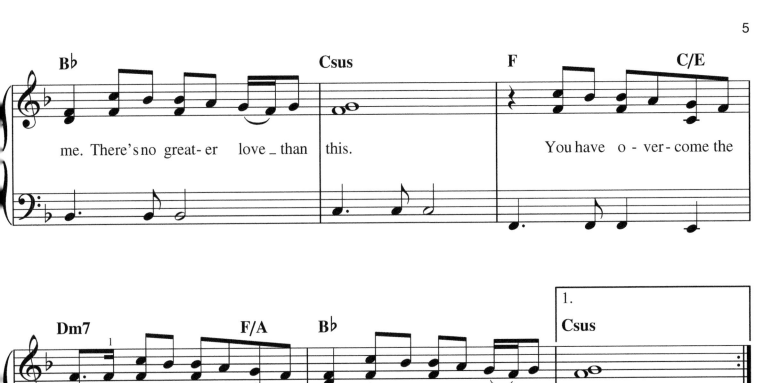

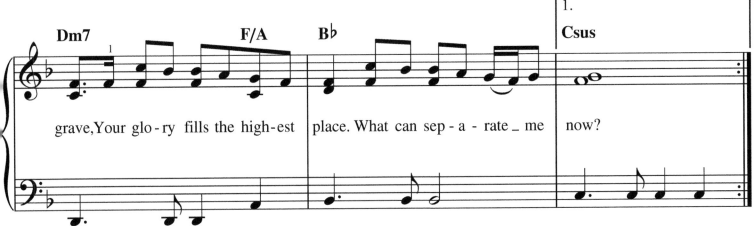

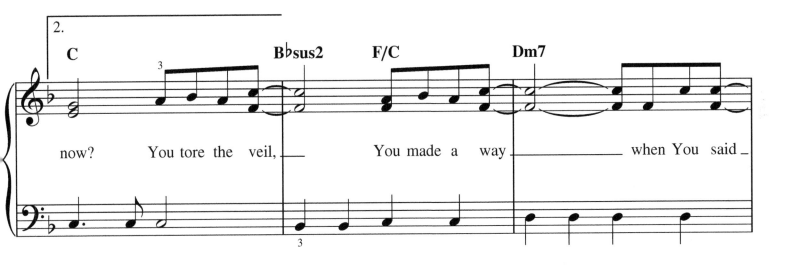

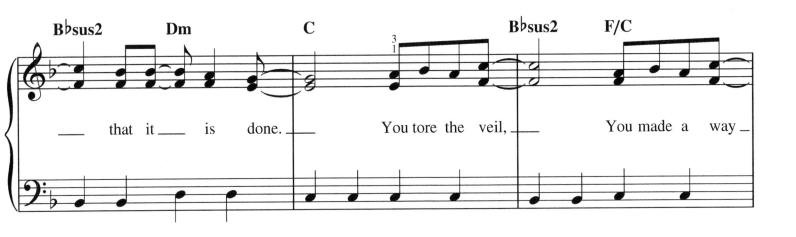

6

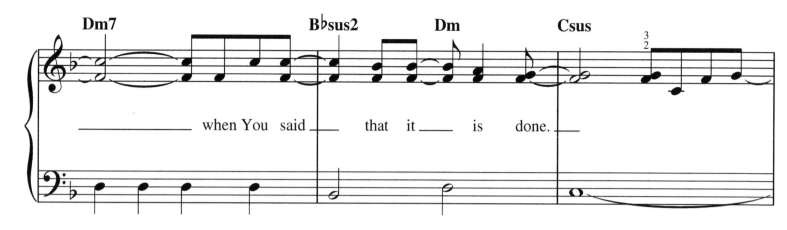

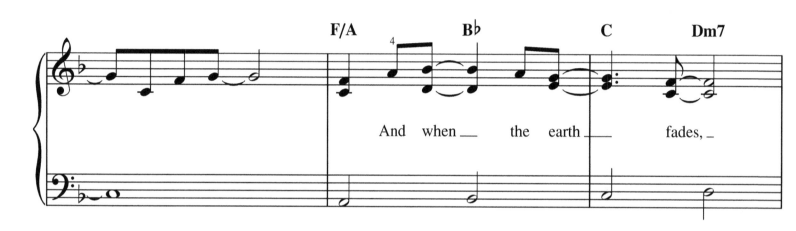

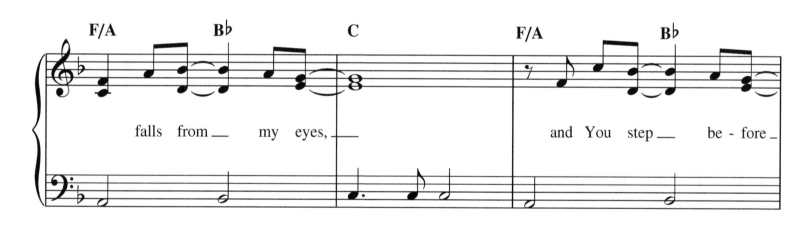

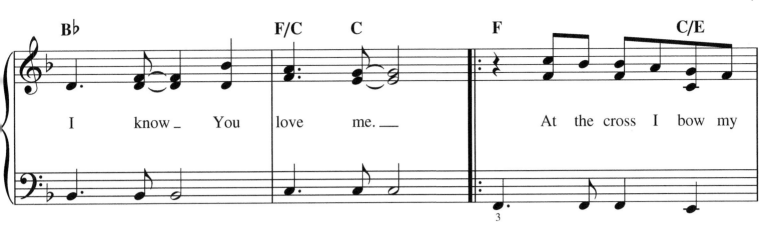

I know _ You love me. _ At the cross I bow my

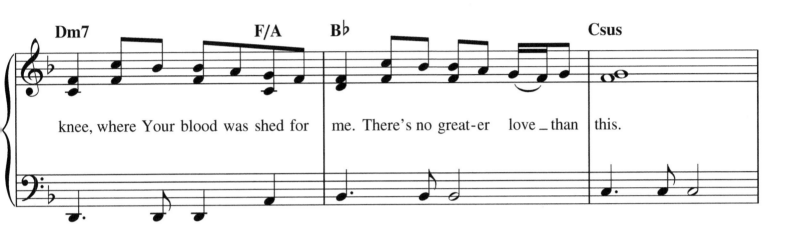

knee, where Your blood was shed for me. There's no great-er love _ than this.

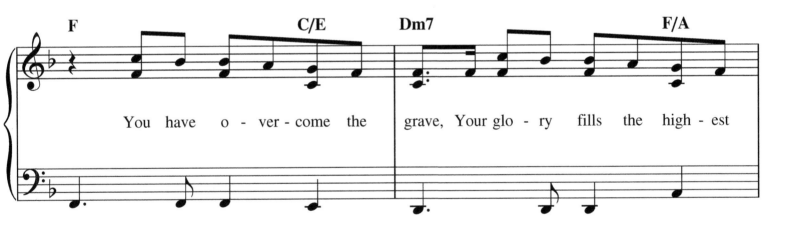

You have o - ver - come the grave, Your glo - ry fills the high - est

place. What can sep - a - rate _ me now? now? You tore the veil, _

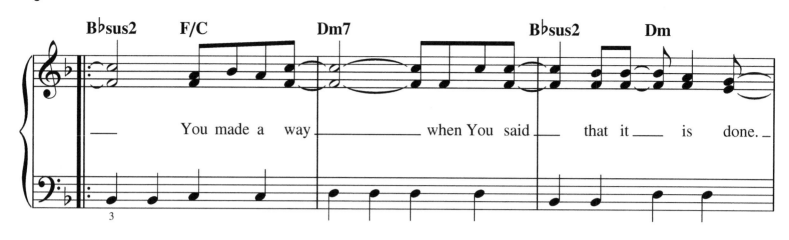

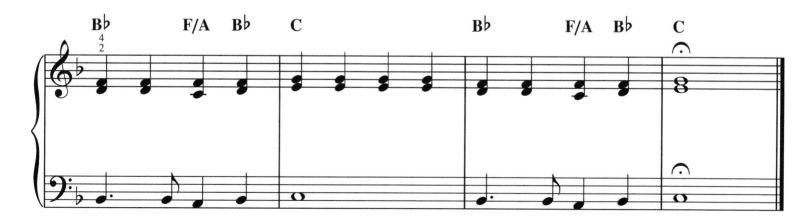

EVERYDAY

Words and Music by
JOEL HOUSTON

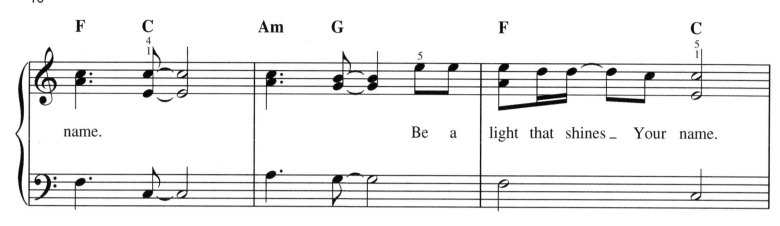

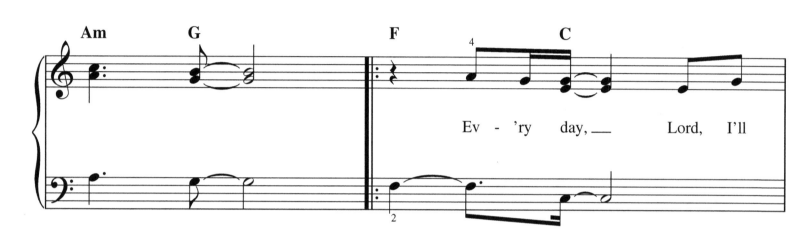

12

CAME TO MY RESCUE

Words and Music by MARTY SAMPSON,
DYLAN THOMAS and JOEL DAVIES

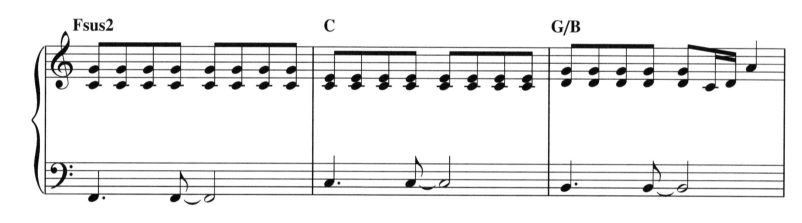

Fall-ing on ___ my knees ___

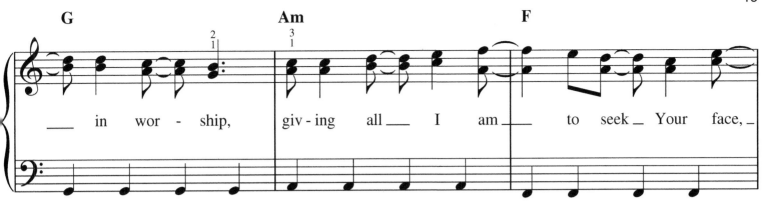

in wor - ship, giv - ing all __ I am __ to seek __ Your face, __

__ Lord, all __ I am __ is Yours. __

My whole life __ I place __ in Your __ hands.

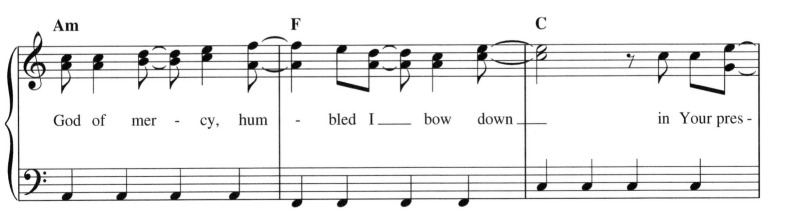

God of mer - cy, hum - bled I __ bow down __ in Your pres -

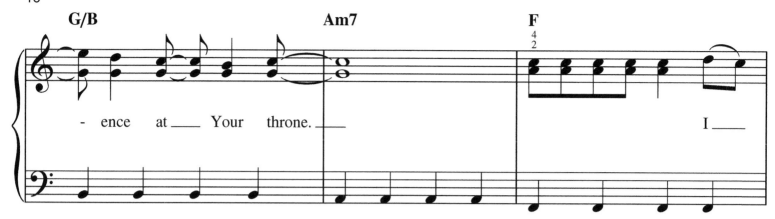

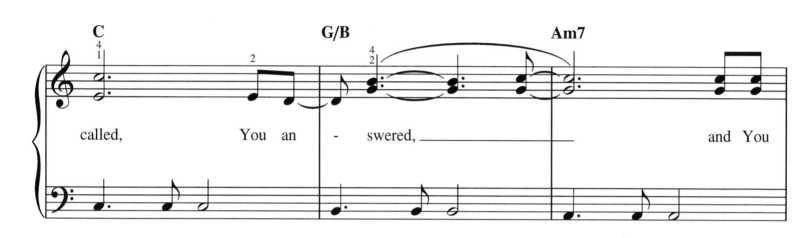

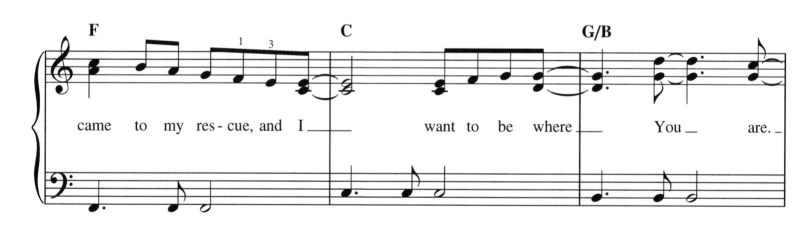

18

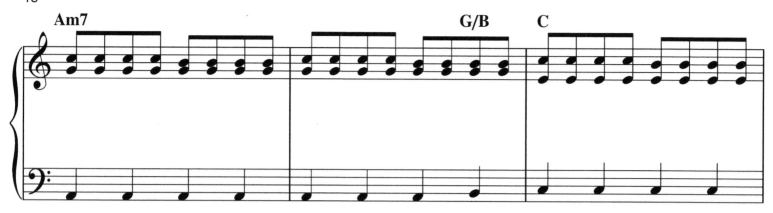

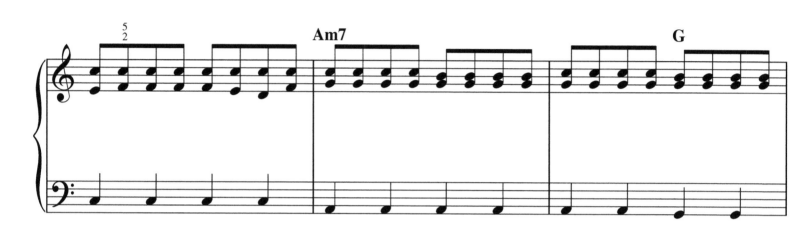

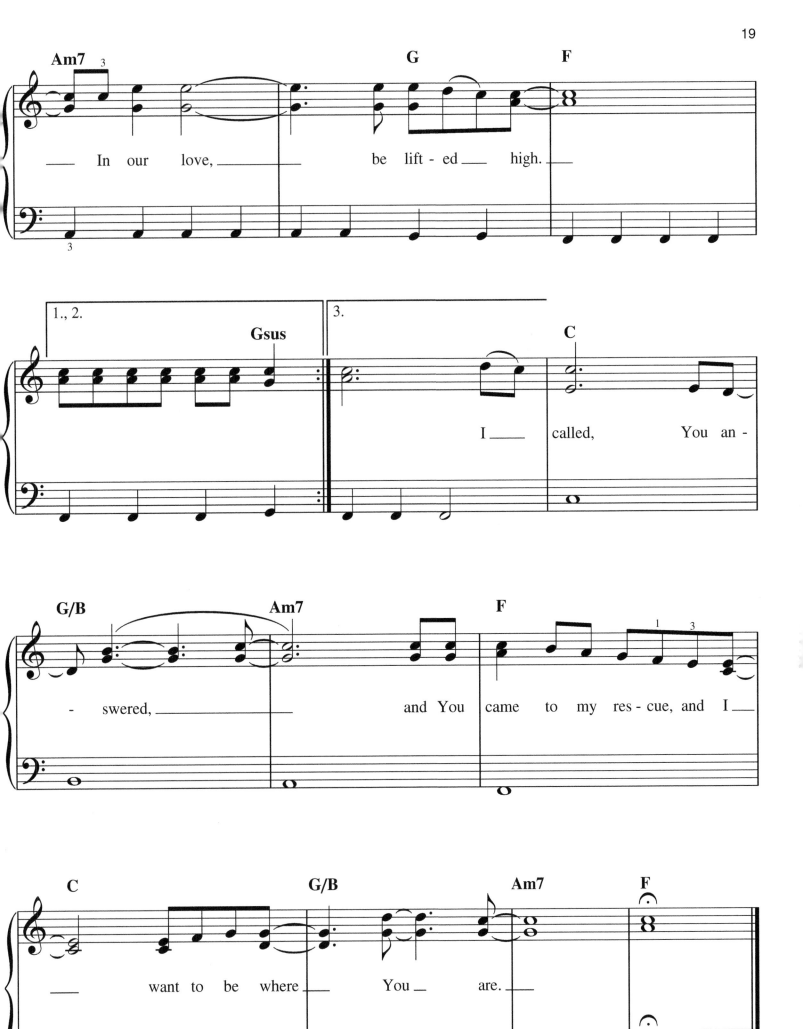

DESERT SONG

Words and Music by
BROOKE FRASER

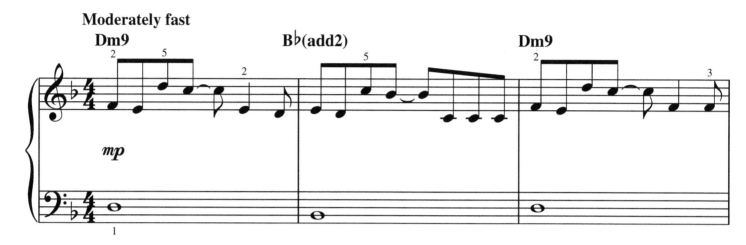

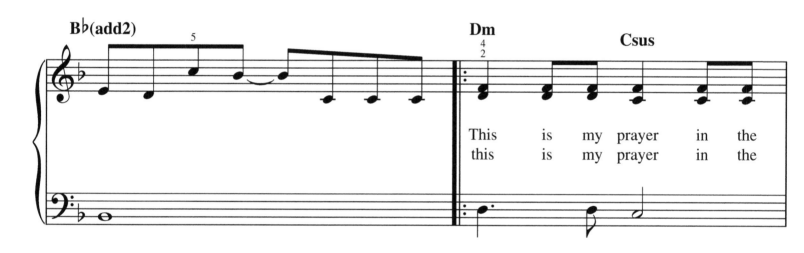

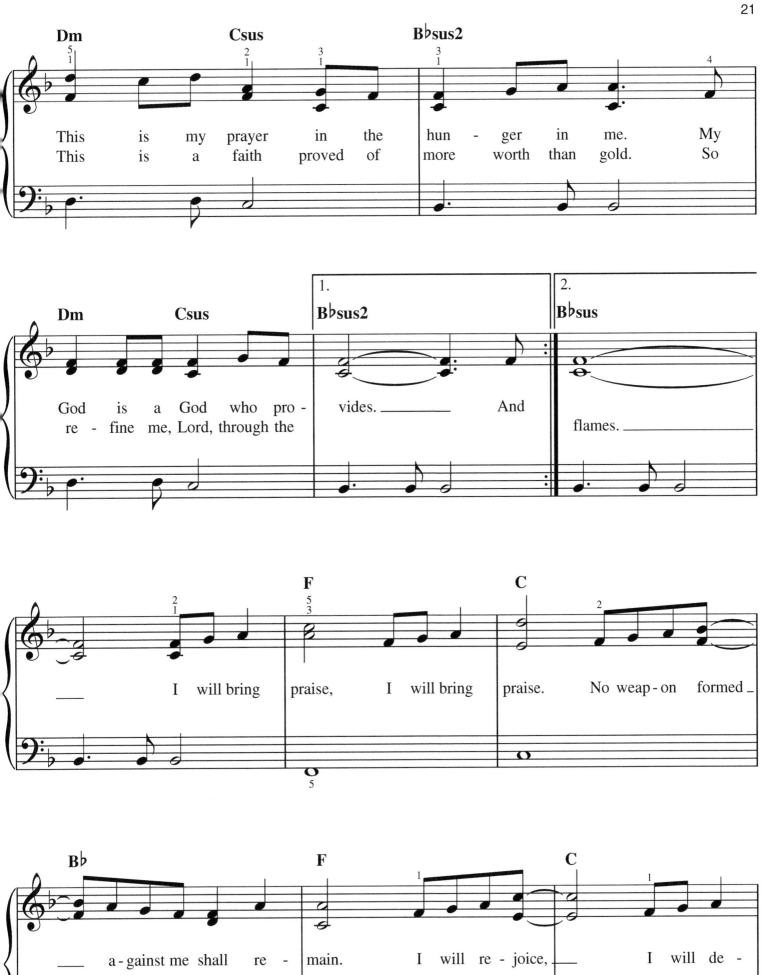

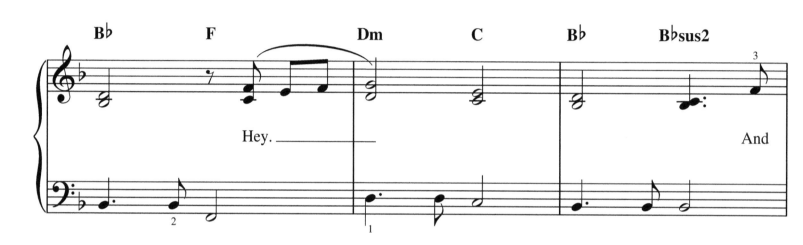

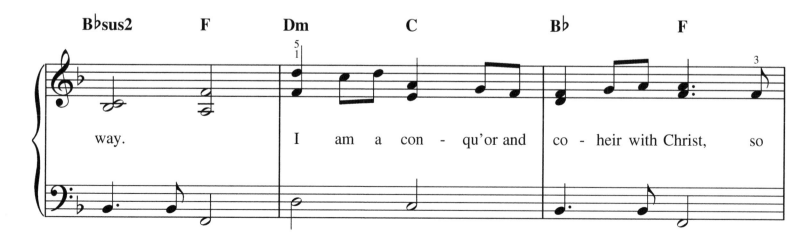

23

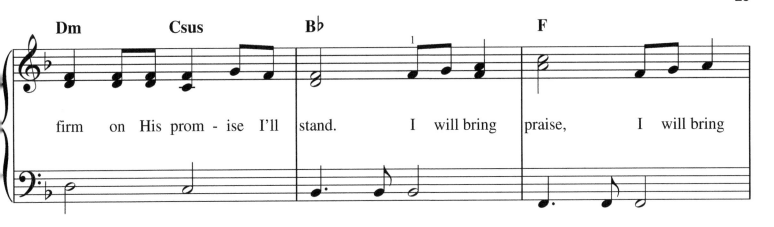

firm on His prom - ise I'll stand. I will bring praise, I will bring

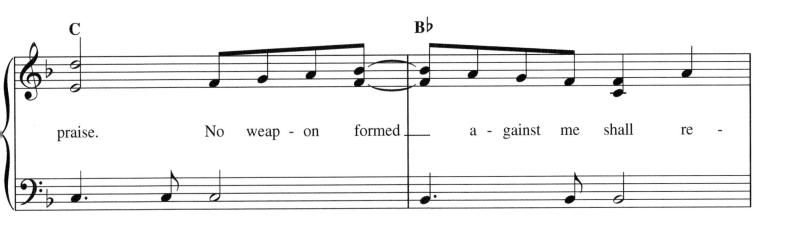

praise. No weap - on formed a - gainst me shall re -

main. I will re - joice, I will de - clare: God is my vic -

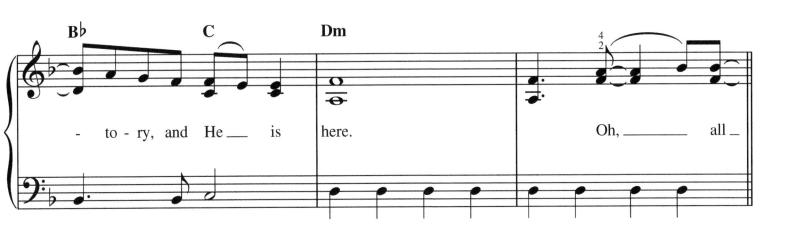

- to - ry, and He is here. Oh, all

24

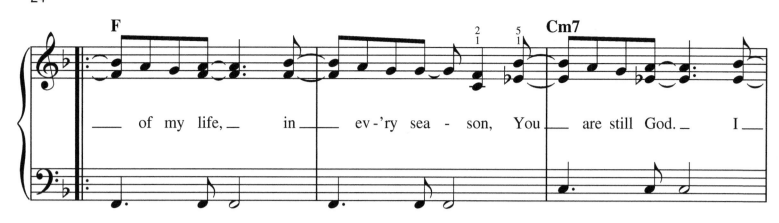

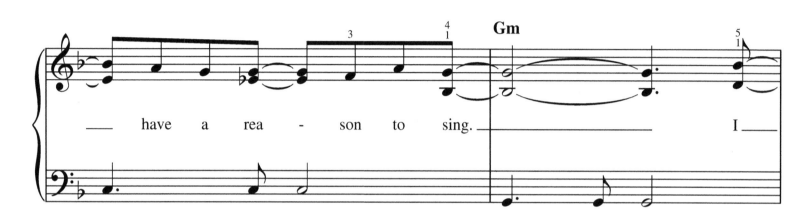

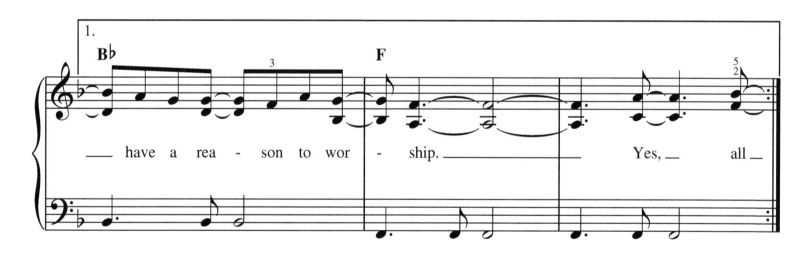

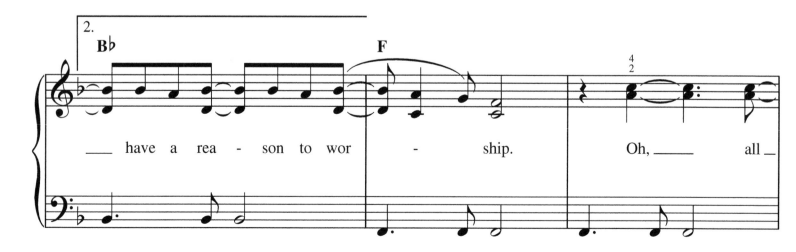

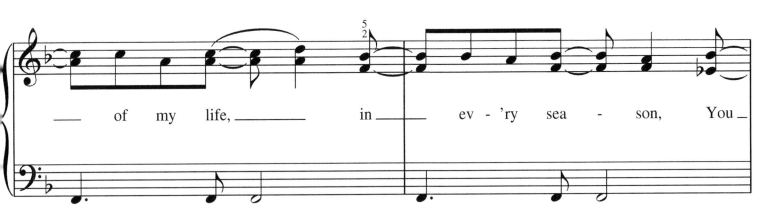

_ of my life, _____ in ___ ev - 'ry sea - son, You _

Cm7

_ are still God. _ I ___ have a rea - son to sing. _____ **Gm** I _

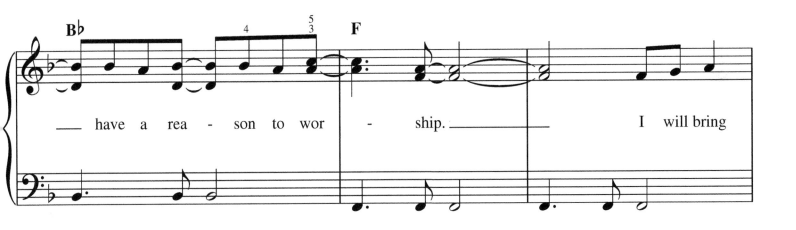

B♭

_ have a rea - son to wor - ship. _____ **F** I will bring

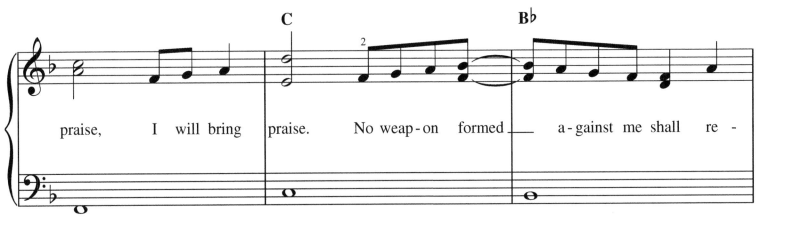

praise, I will bring praise. **C** No weap-on formed ___ a-gainst me shall re - **B♭**

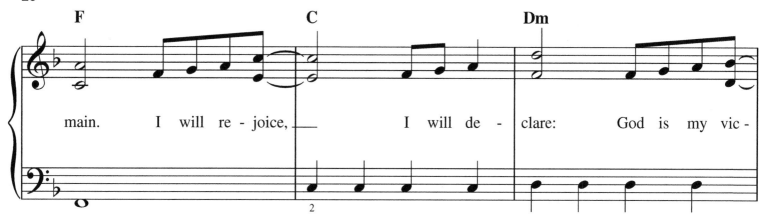

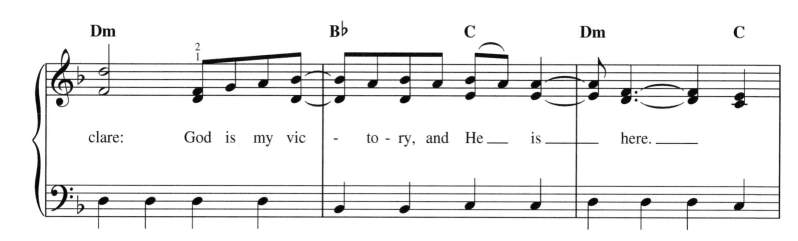

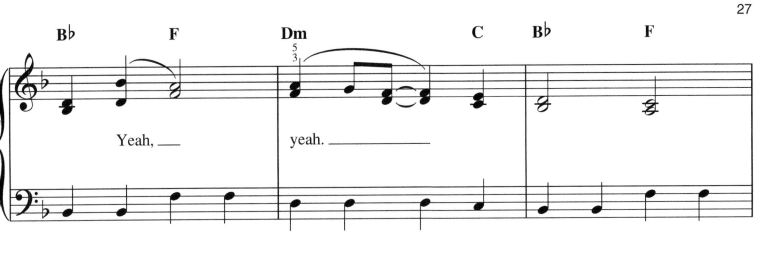

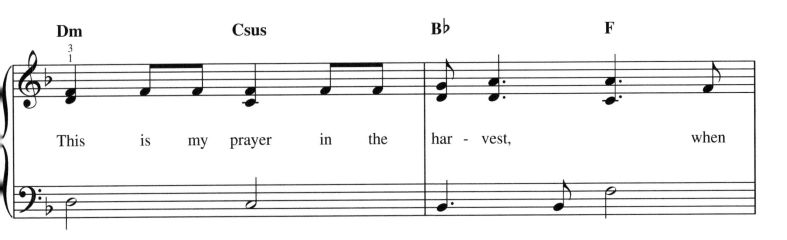

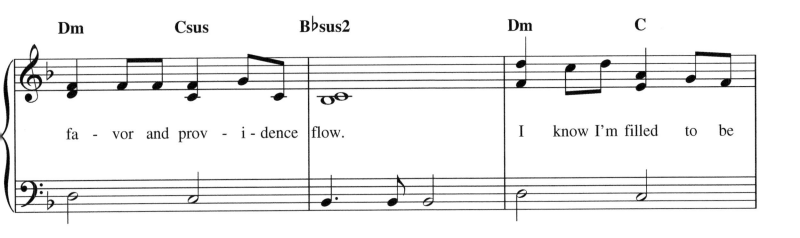

FROM THE INSIDE OUT

Words and Music by
JOEL HOUSTON

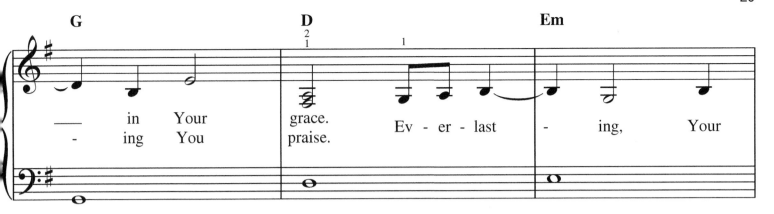

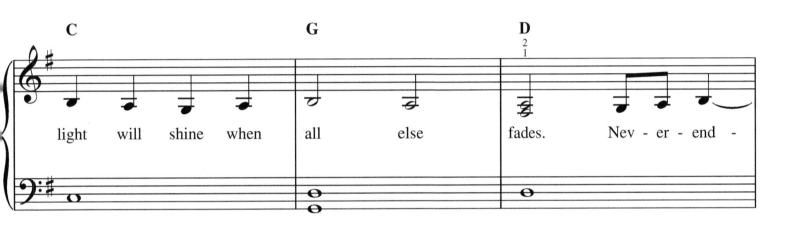

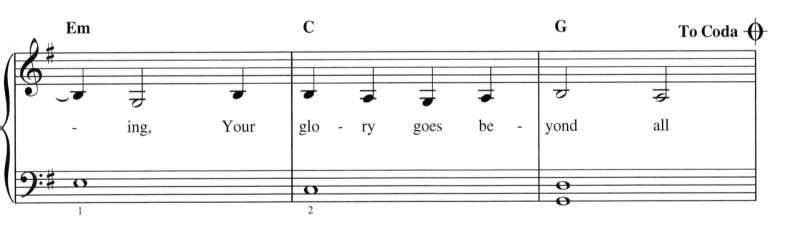

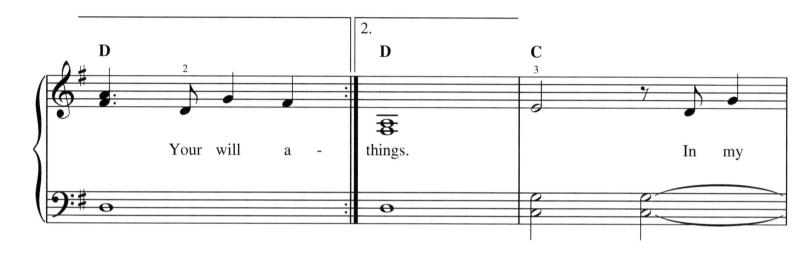

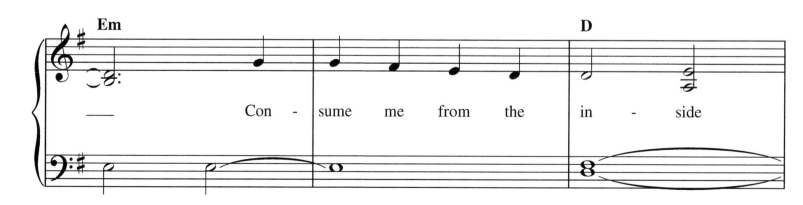

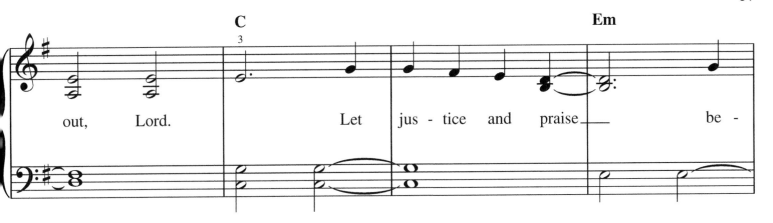

out, Lord. Let jus - tice and praise___ be -

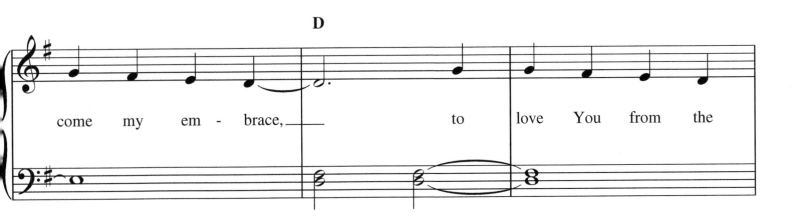

come my em - brace,___ to love You from the

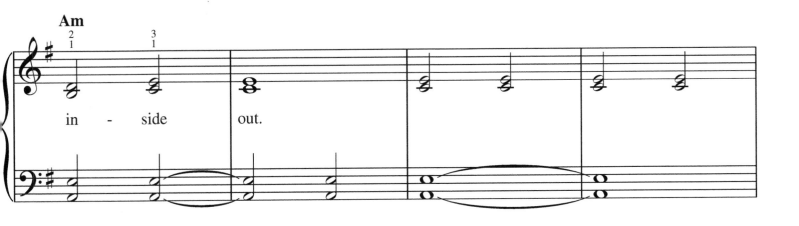

in - side out.

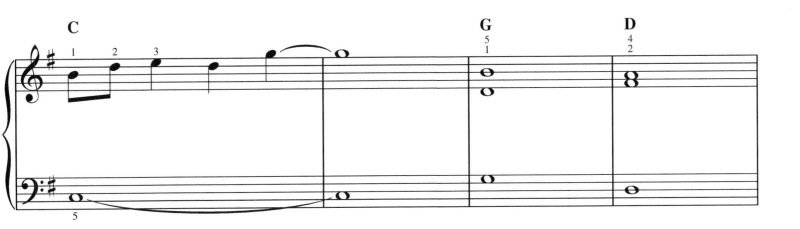

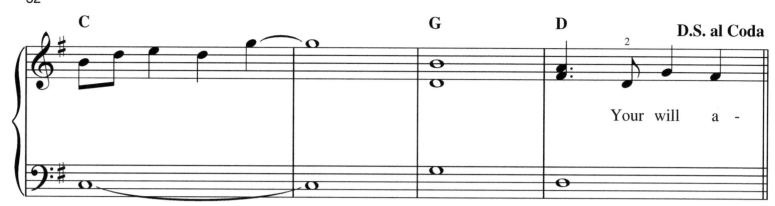

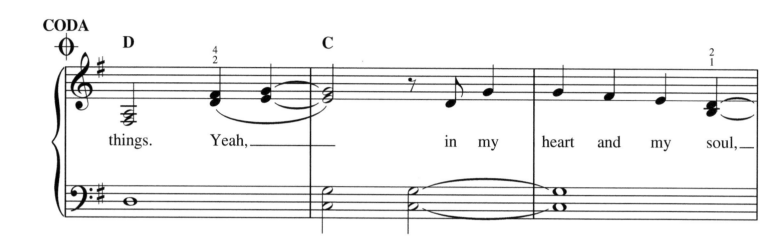

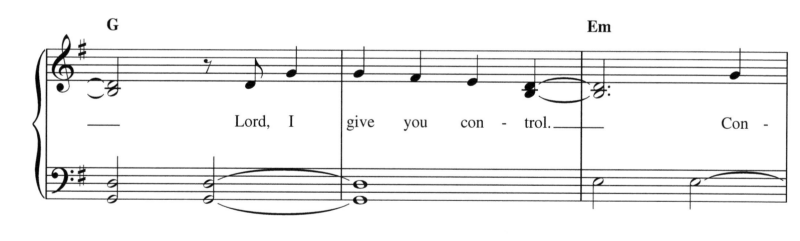

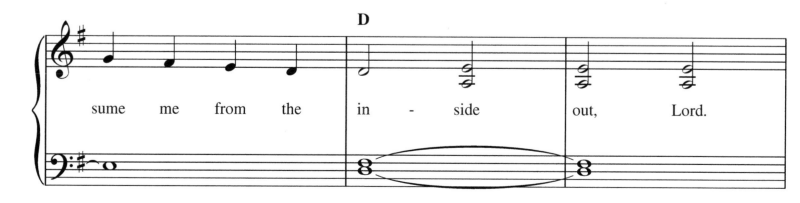

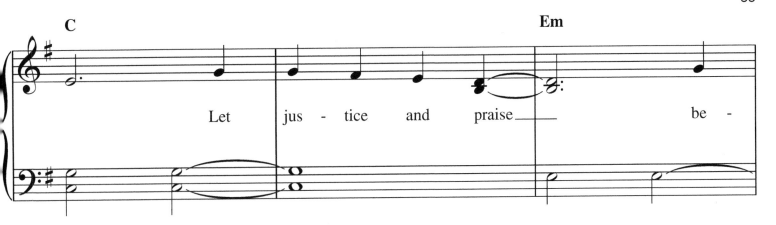

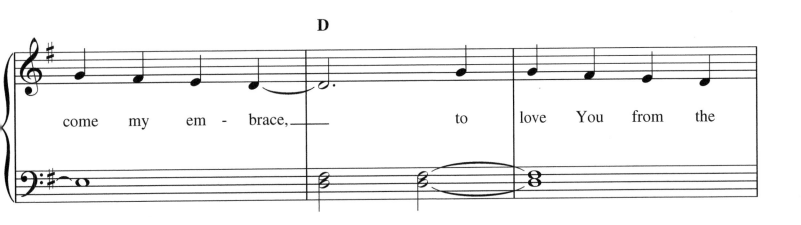

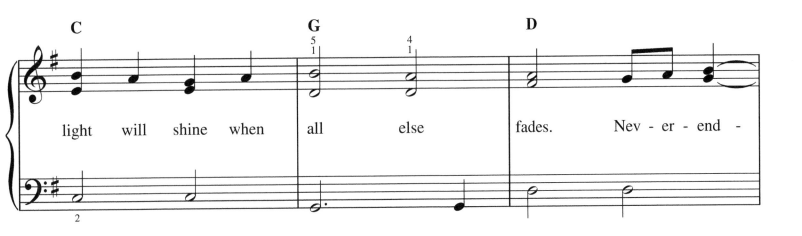

34

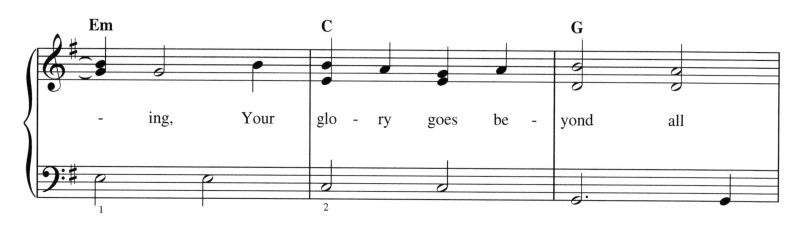

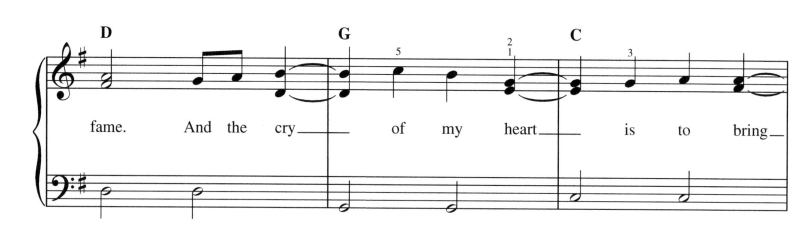

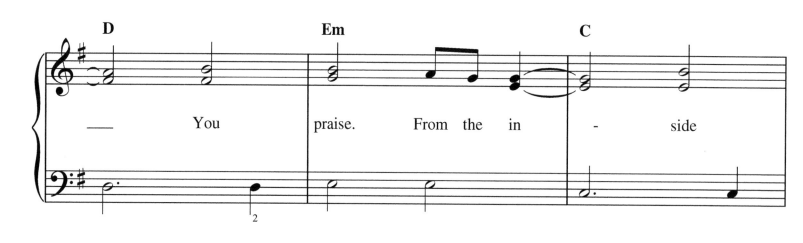

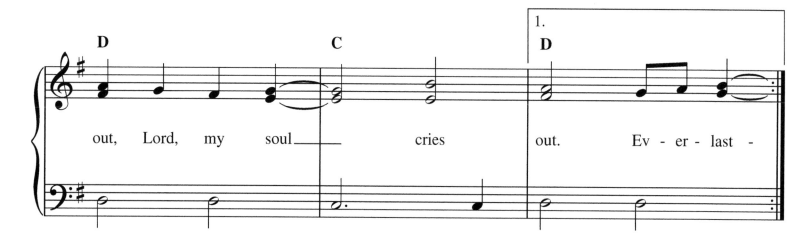

out. From the in - side out, Lord, my soul___

___ cries out, Lord._____

rit.

GOD IS GREAT

Words and Music by
MARTY SAMPSON

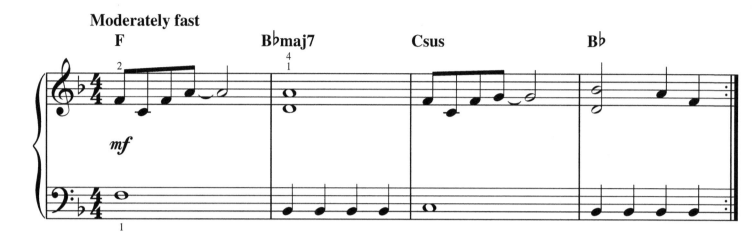

All__ cre - a - tion cries__ to You,
All__ cre - a - tion gives__ You praise.

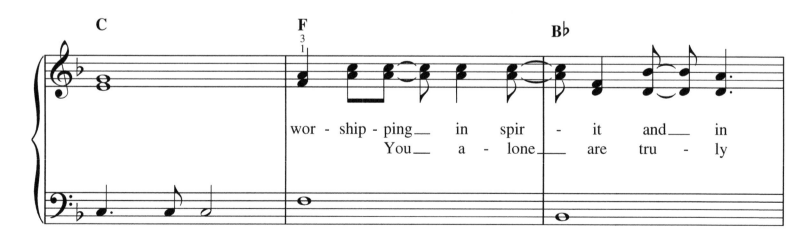

wor - ship - ping__ in spir - it and__ in
You__ a - lone__ are tru - ly

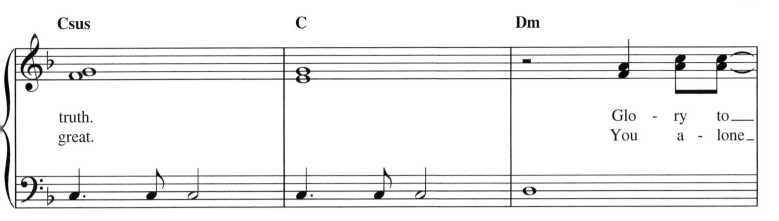

truth.
great.

Glo - ry to___
You a - lone_

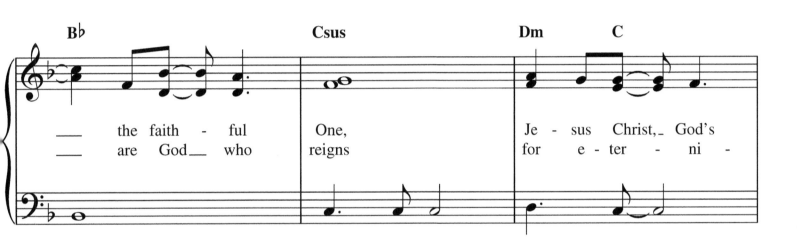

___ the faith - ful
___ are God__ who

One,
reigns

Je - sus Christ,_ God's
for e - ter - ni -

Son.
ty.

1.

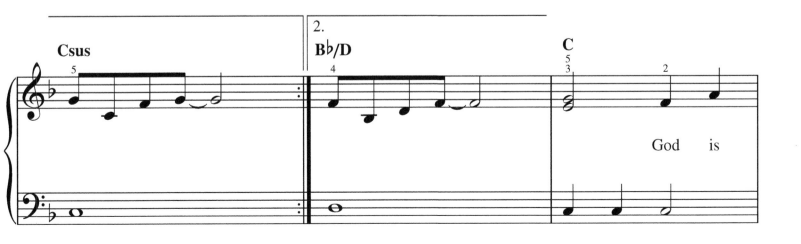

2.

God is

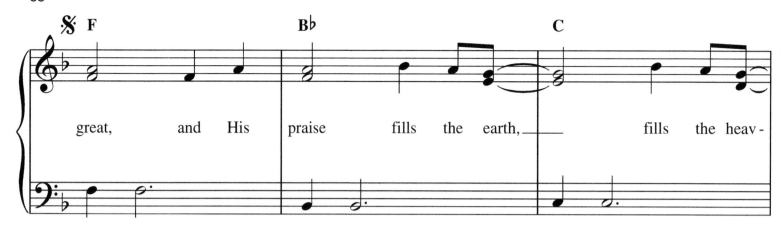

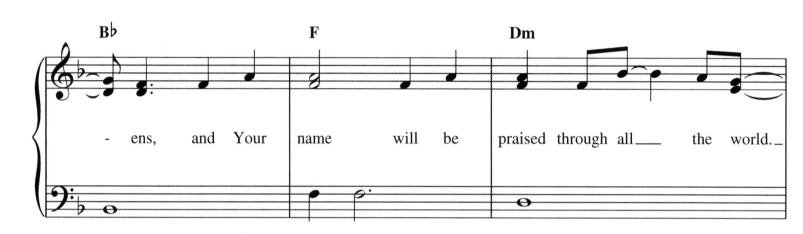

liv - ing for __ the glo - ry of __ Your name, ____ the

glo - ry of __ Your name. __

To Coda ⊕

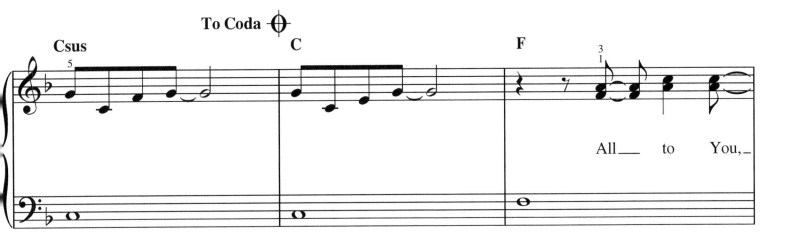

All __ to You, _

__ O God, __ we bring.

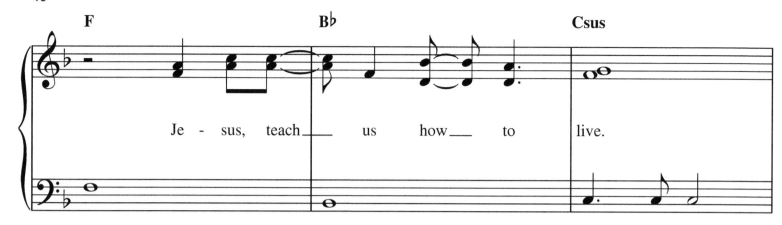

Je - sus, teach___ us how___ to live.

Let Your fi - re burn___ in

us_____ that all may___ hear,

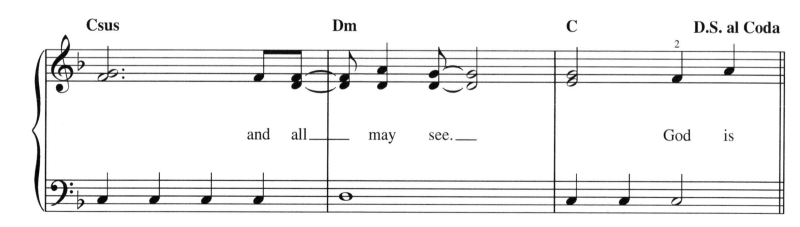

D.S. al Coda

and all___ may see.___ God is

41

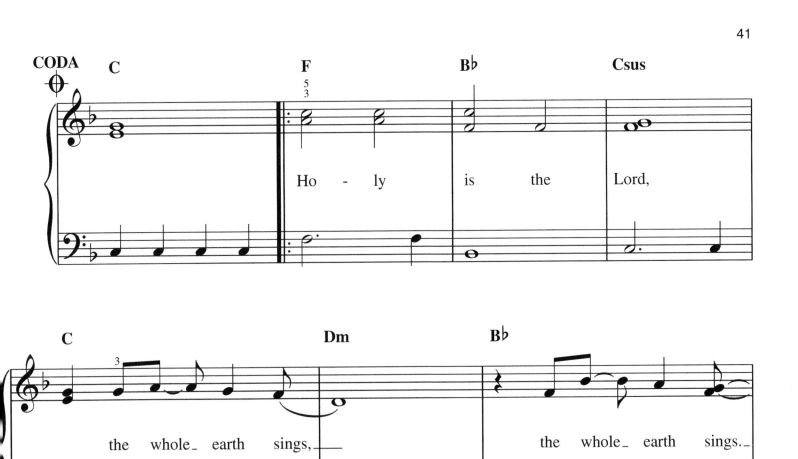

Ho - ly   is   the   Lord,

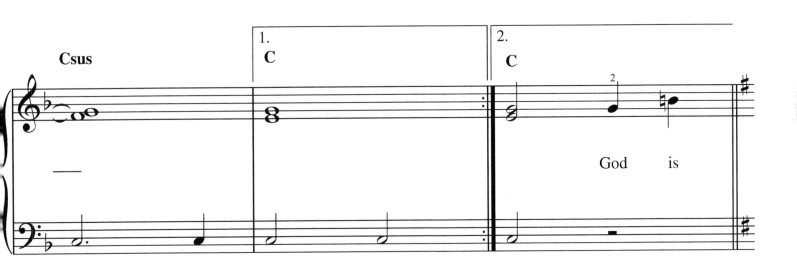

the whole earth sings,____   the whole earth sings.__

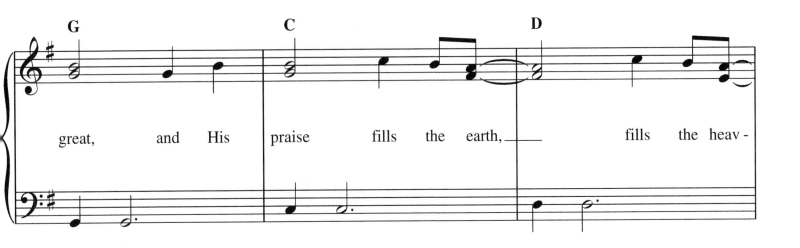

1.
2.

____   God is

great,   and His   praise fills the earth,____   fills the heav -

42

'Cause we're liv - ing for___ the glo - ry of___ Your name,___

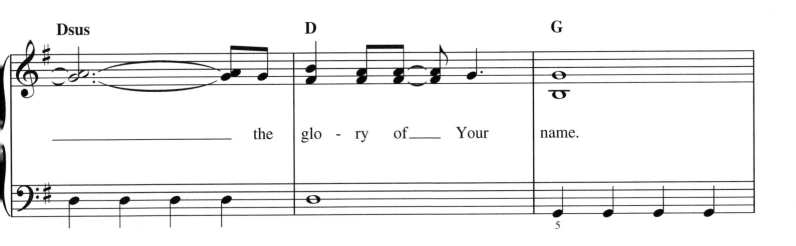

_____ the glo - ry of___ Your name.

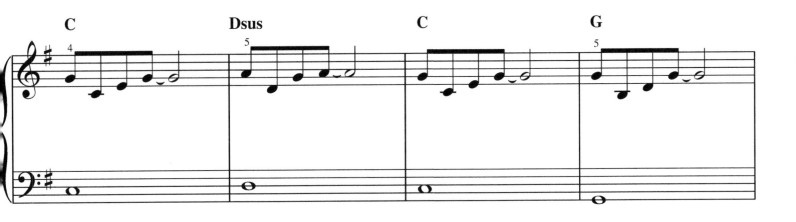

HEAR OUR PRAISES

Words and Music by
REUBEN MORGAN

With energy

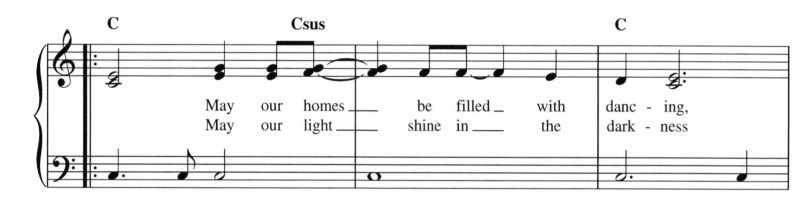

May our homes ___ be filled ___ with the danc - ing,
May our light ___ shine in ___ with the dark - ness

may our streets ___ be filled ___ with
as we walk ___ be - fore ___ the

joy.   May in - jus -
cross.   May Your glo -

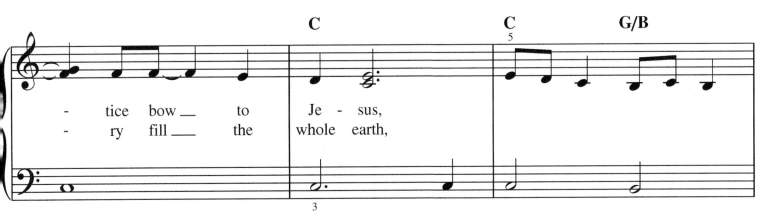

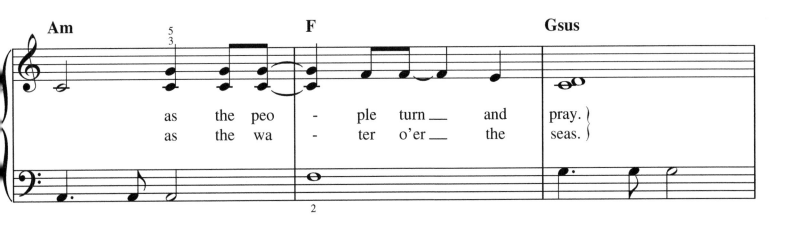

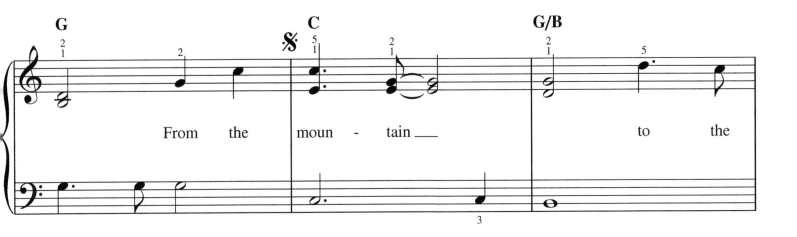

46

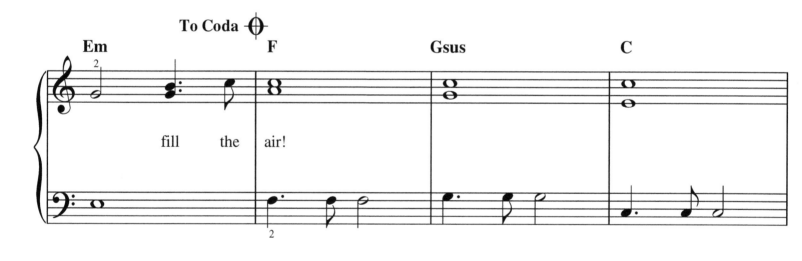

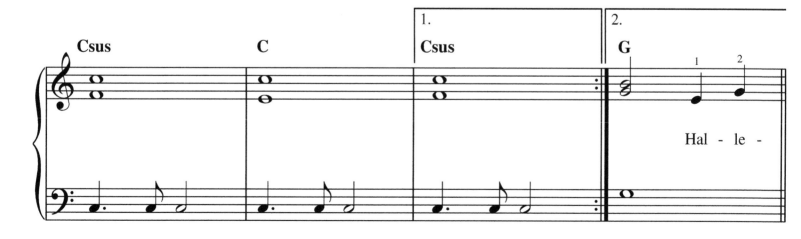

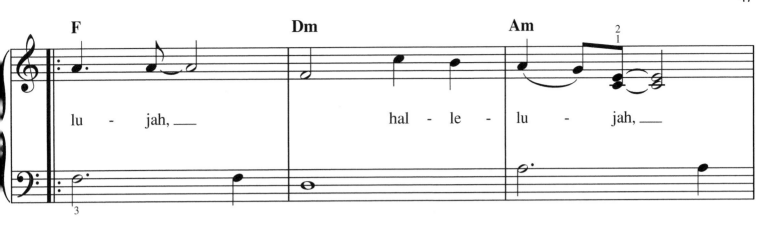

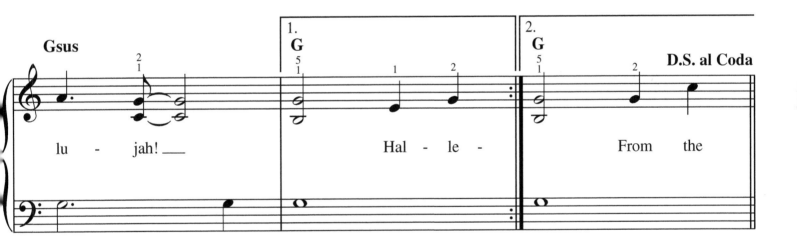

HOLY SPIRIT RAIN DOWN

Words and Music by
RUSSELL FRAGAR

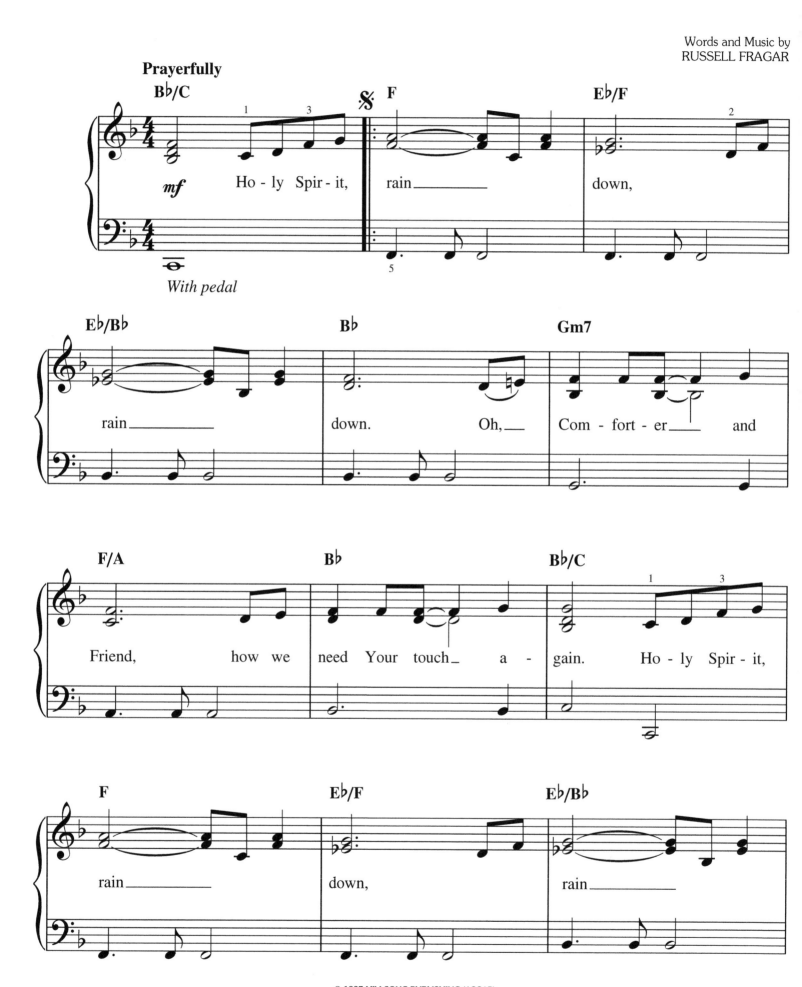

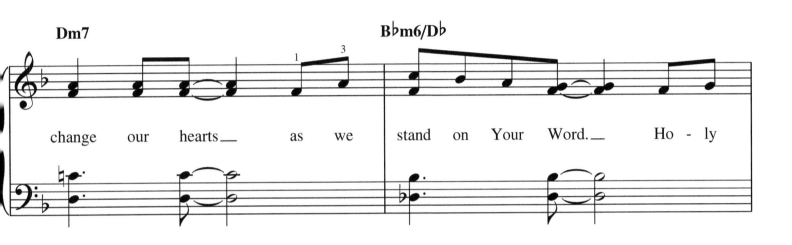

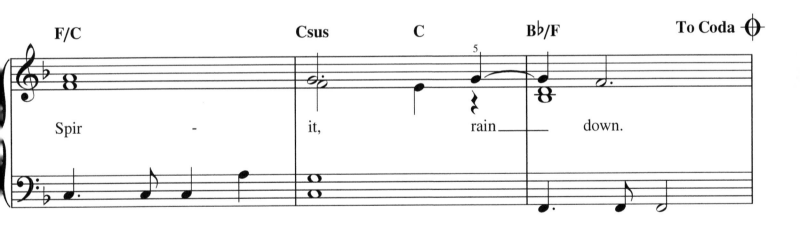

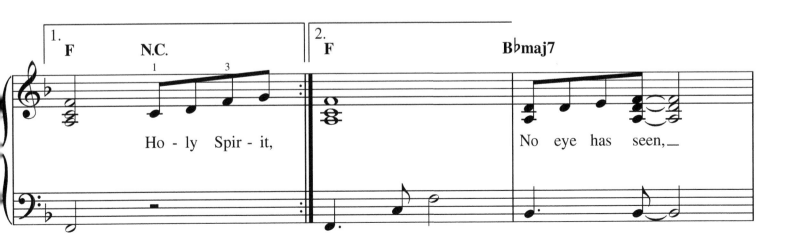

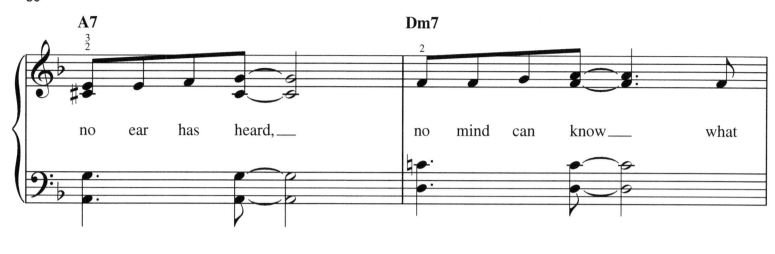

no ear has heard, ___ no mind can know ___ what

God has in store. ___ So o - pen up heav - en,

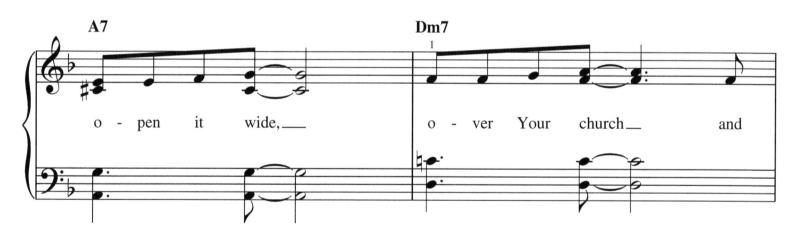

o - pen it wide, ___ o - ver Your church ___ and

o - ver our lives. ___ Ho - ly Spir - it,

D.S. al Coda

CODA

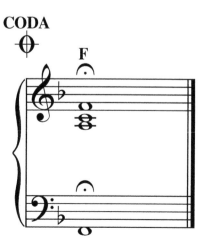

I GIVE YOU MY HEART

Words and Music by
REUBEN MORGAN

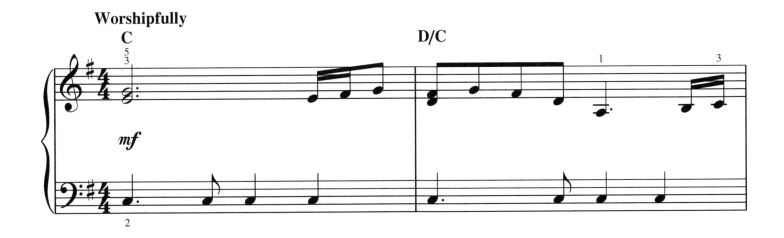

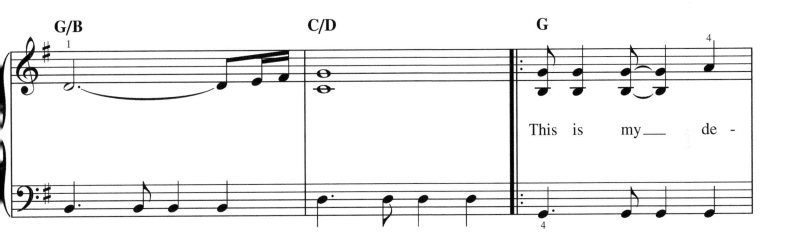

This is my ___ de -

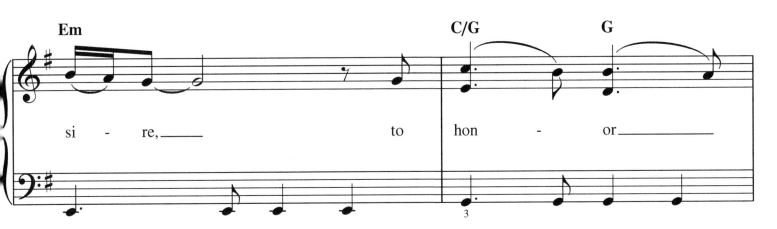

si - re, ___ to hon - or ___

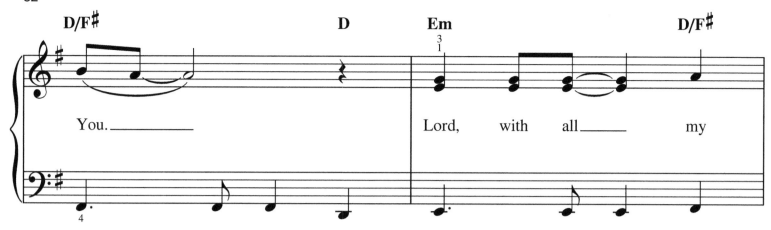

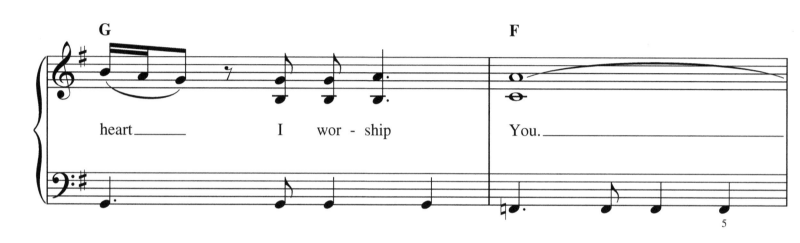

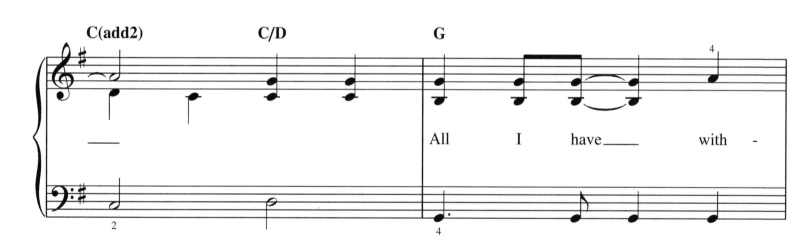

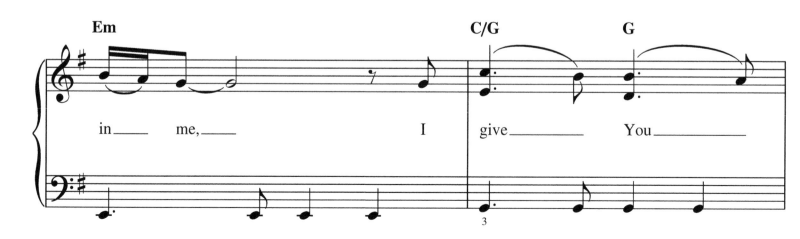

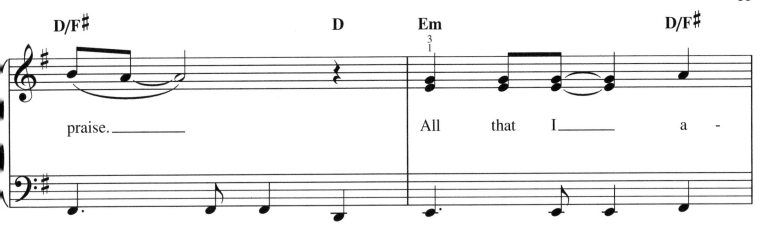

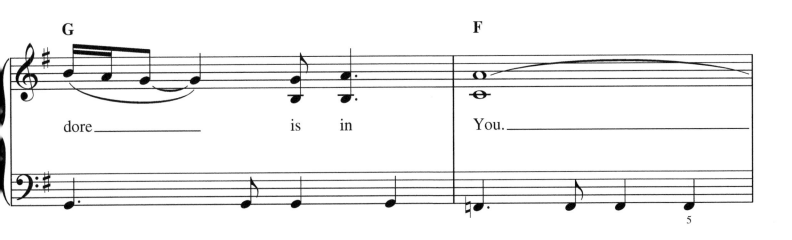

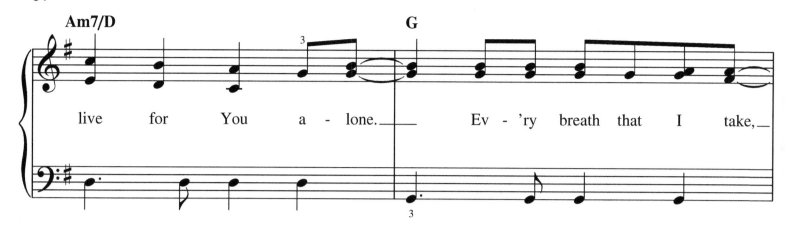

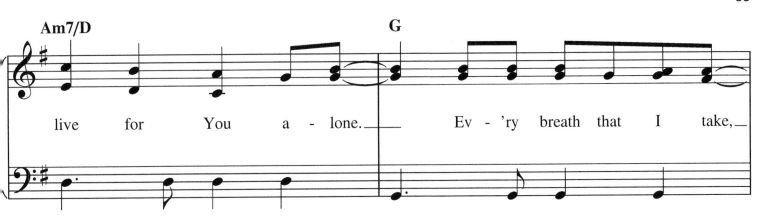

live for You a - lone.___ Ev - 'ry breath that I take,___

___ ev - 'ry mo - ment I'm a - wake,___ Lord,

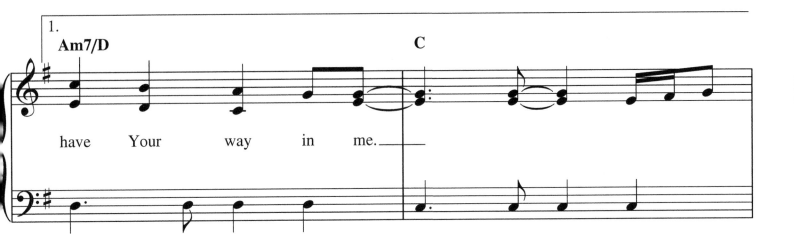

1.

have Your way in me.___

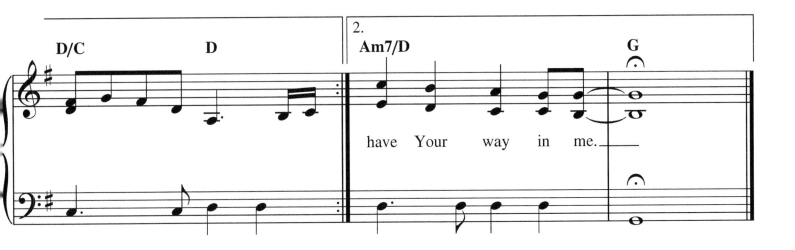

2.

have Your way in me.___

HOSANNA

Words and Music by
BROOKE FRASER

I see the King of Glo - ry _____

com - ing on the clouds with fire; _____ the whole earth shakes, _

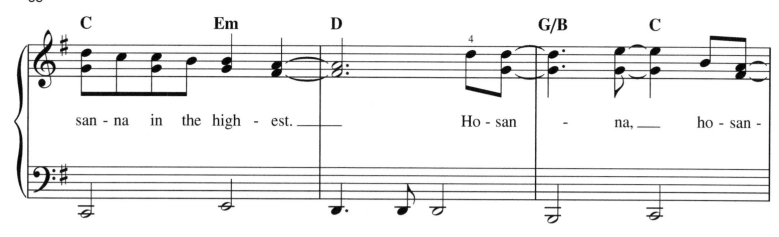

san - na in the high - est. ___ Ho - san - na, ___ ho - san-

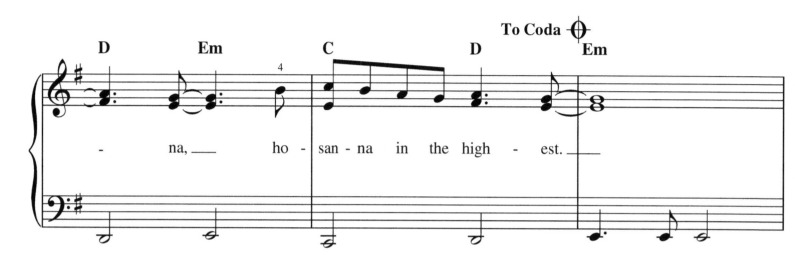

- na, ___ ho - san - na in the high - est. ___

I see a gen - er - a - tion ___

ris - ing up to take their place ___ with self-less faith, ___ with self-less faith. _

59

61

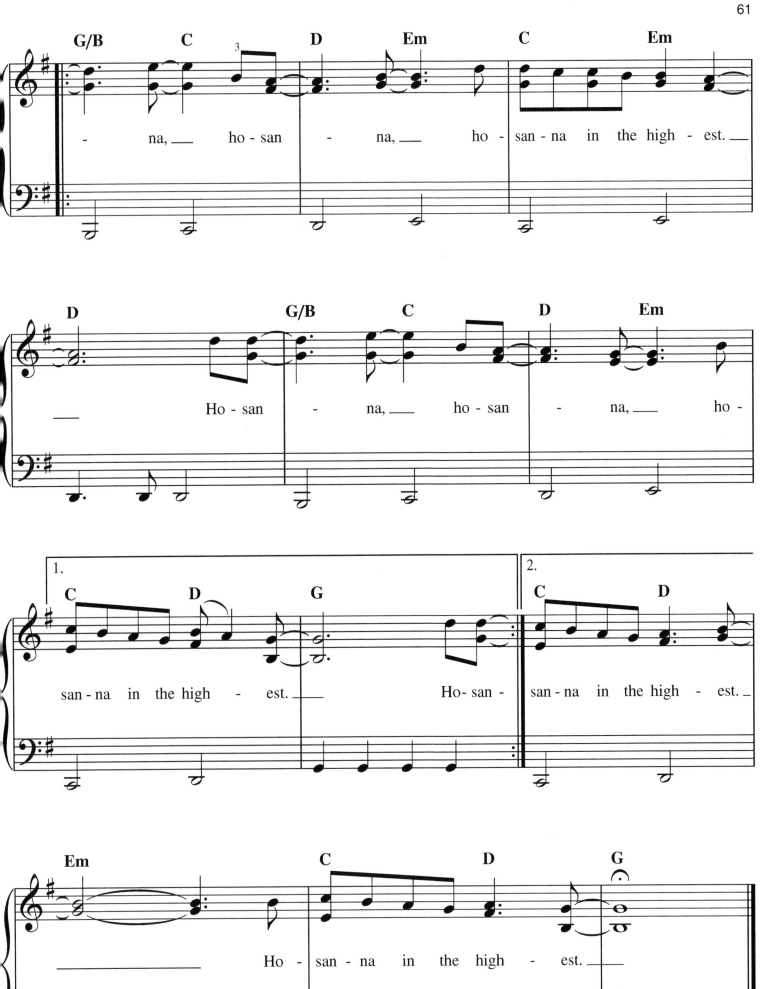

JESUS, LOVER OF MY SOUL

Words and Music by JOHN EZZY,
DANIEL GRUL and STEPHEN McPHERSON

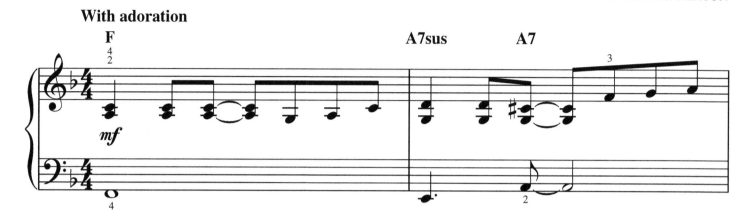

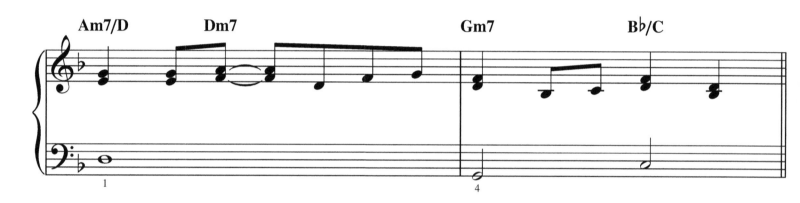

Je - sus,____ lov - er of my soul;____

Je - sus,____ I will nev - er let You go.____

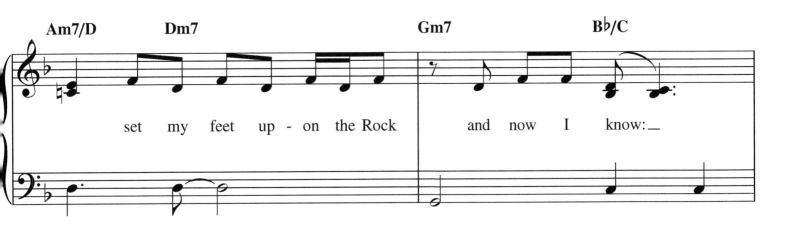

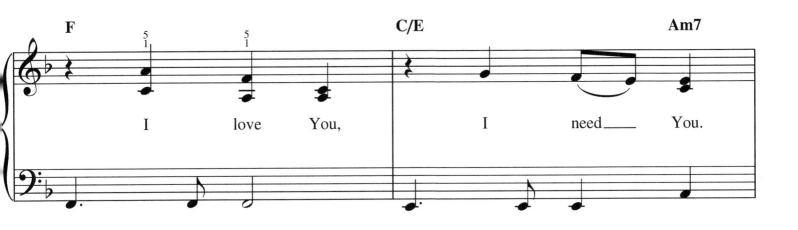

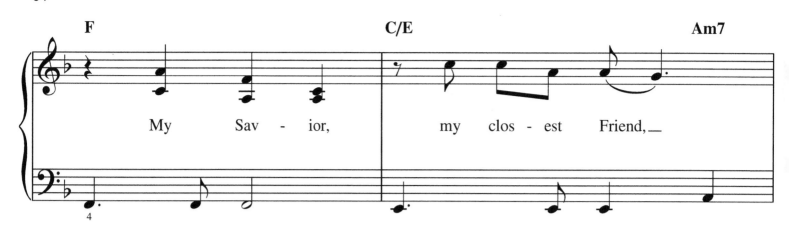

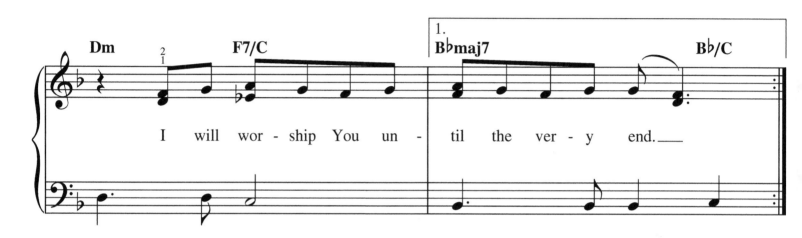

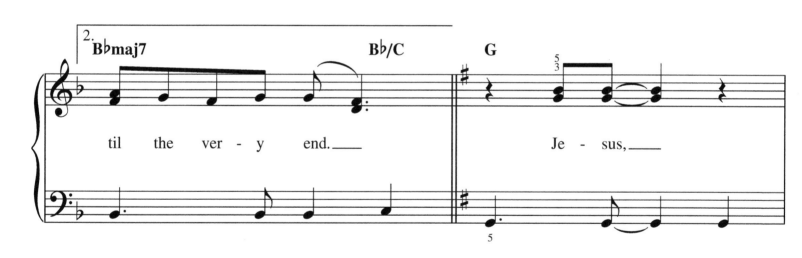

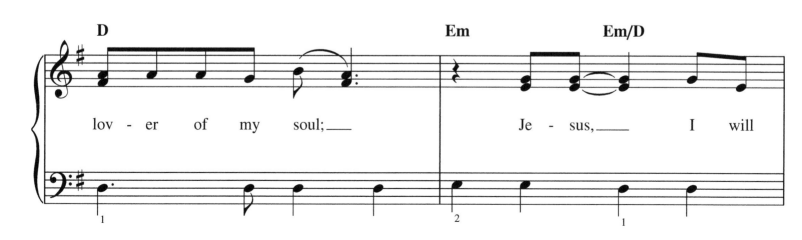

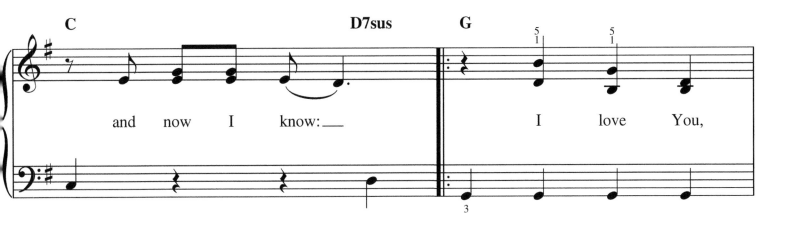

66

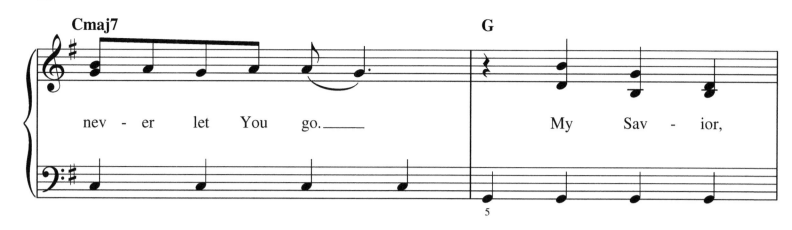

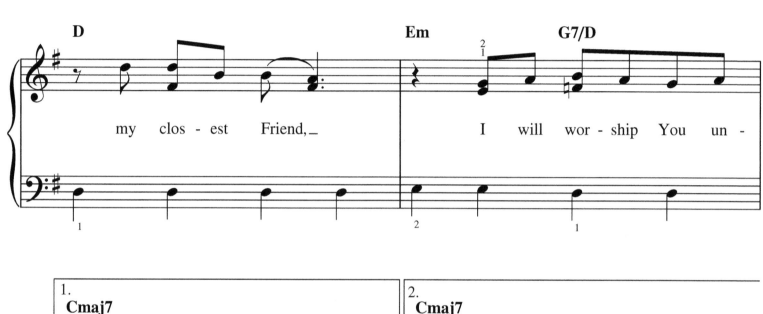

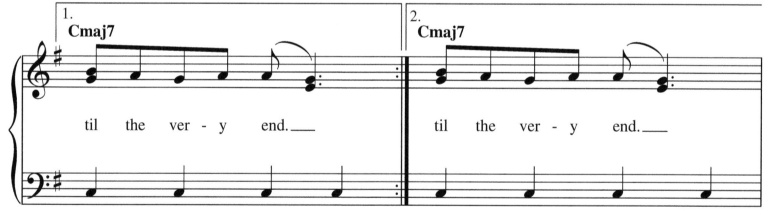

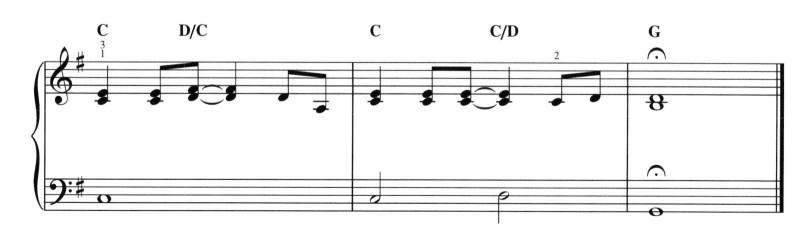

MY REDEEMER LIVES

Words and Music by
REUBEN MORGAN

lieve, _____ I be - lieve. _

My shame He's tak - en a - way. _

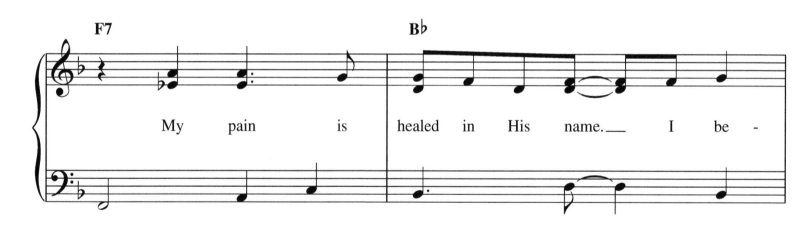

My pain is healed in His name. _ I be -

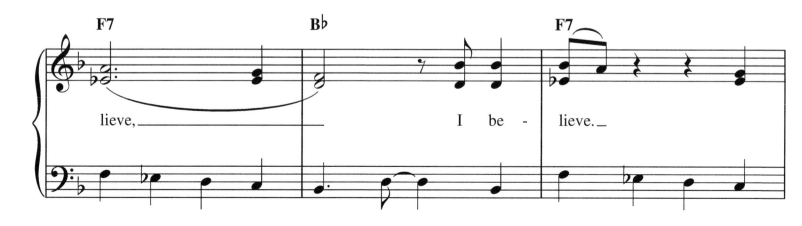

lieve, _____ I be - lieve. _

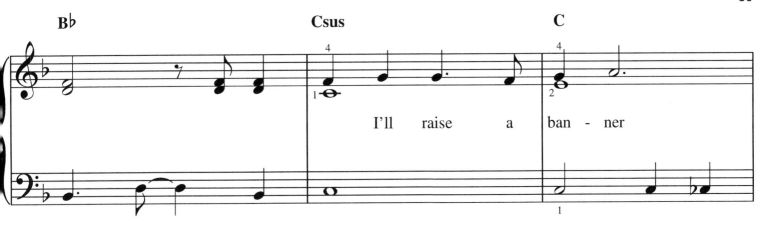

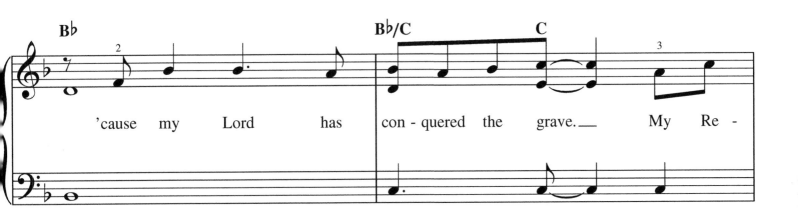

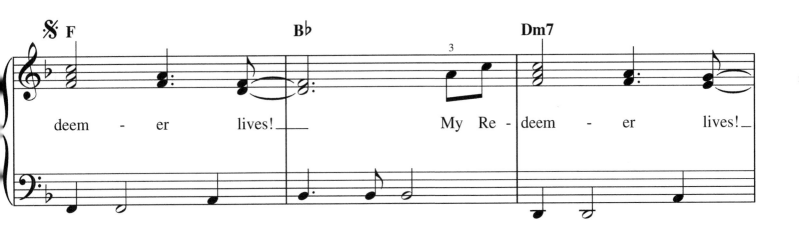

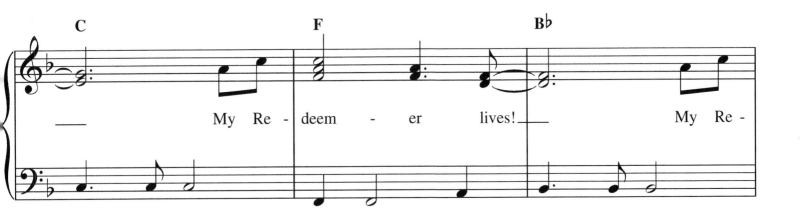

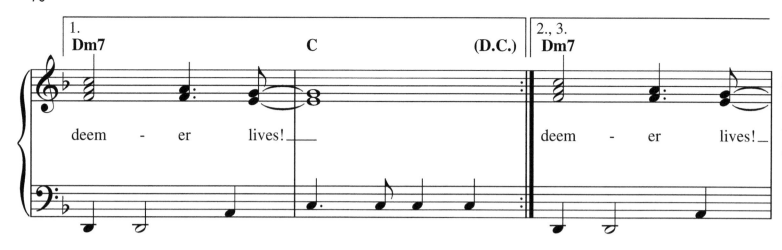

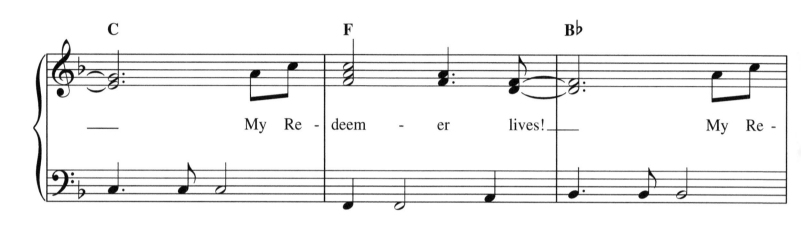

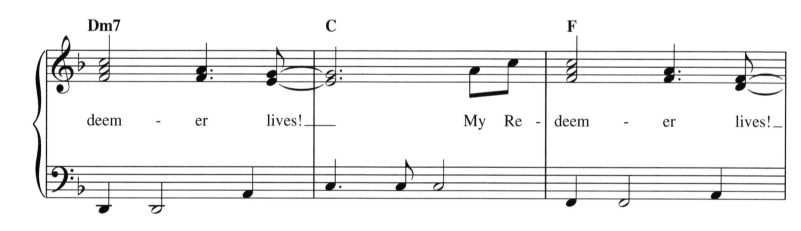

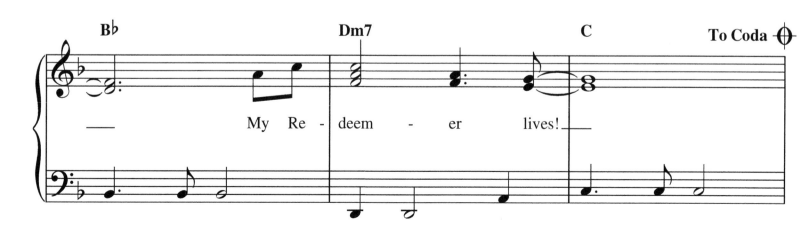

You lift my bur - den

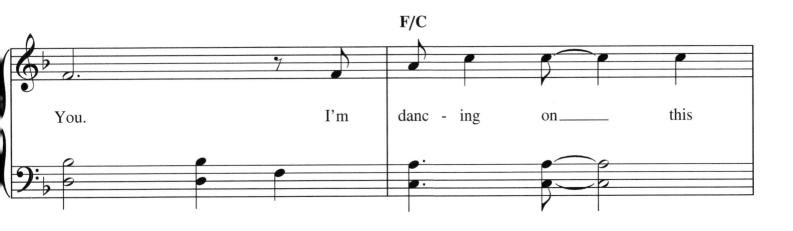

and I rise with You.

I'm danc - ing on _____ this

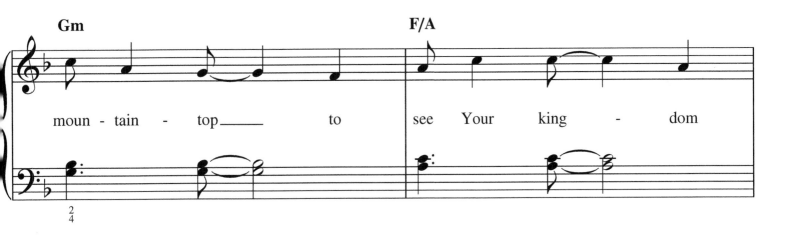

moun - tain - top _____ to see Your king - dom

come.

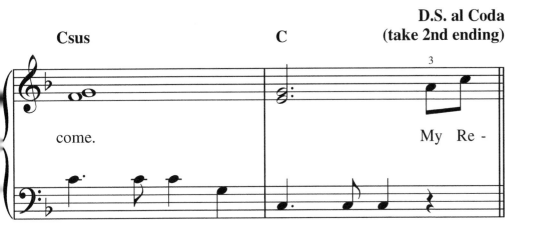

My Re -

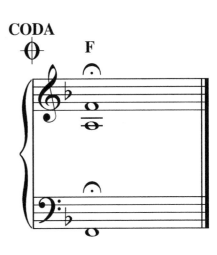

LEAD ME TO THE CROSS

Words and Music by
BROOKE FRASER

Moderate Rock beat

Sav - ior, I come.___ I qui - et my soul,_

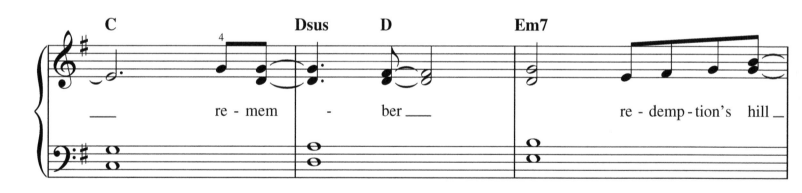

___ re - mem - ber ___ re - demp-tion's hill _

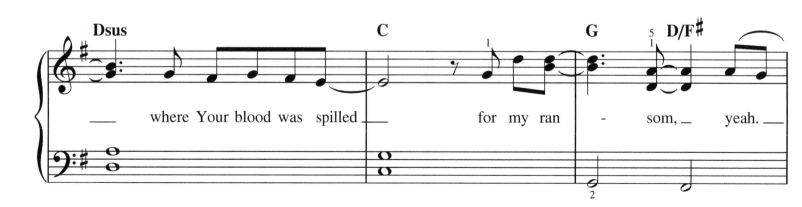

___ where Your blood was spilled ___ for my ran - som,_ yeah.

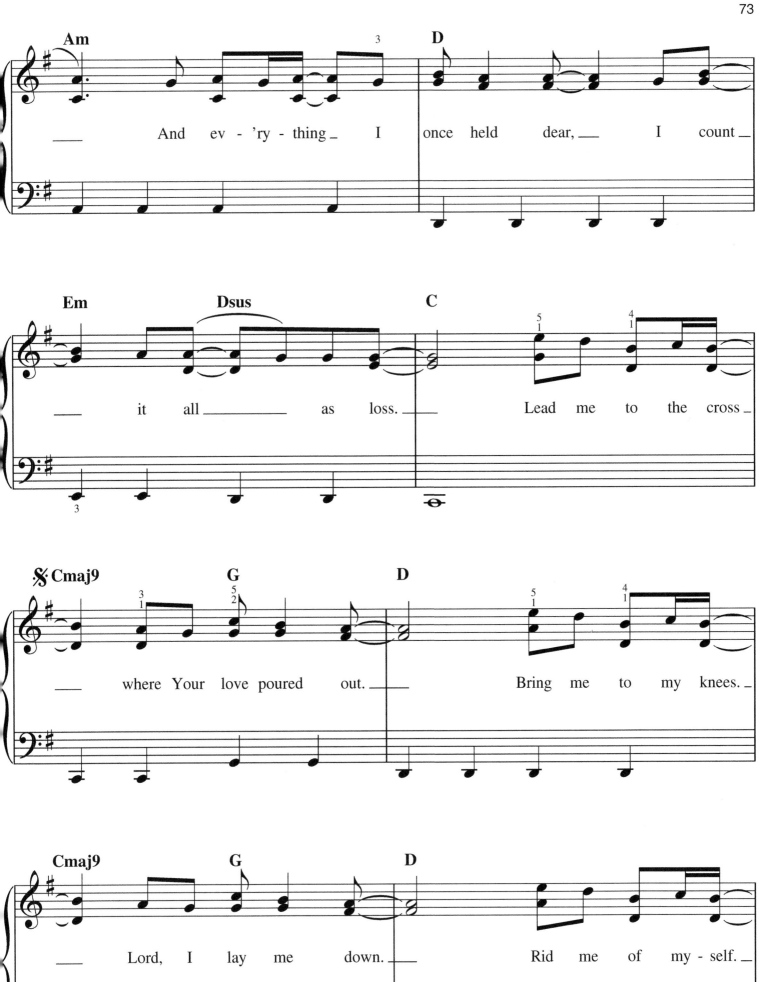

74

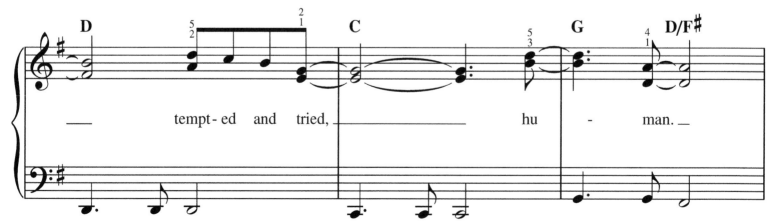

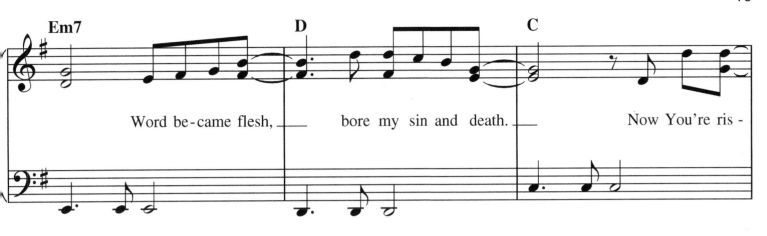

Word be-came flesh, ___ bore my sin and death. ___ Now You're ris -

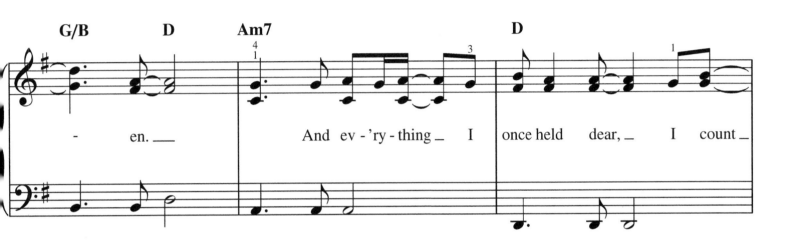

- en. ___ And ev-'ry-thing ___ I once held dear, ___ I count ___

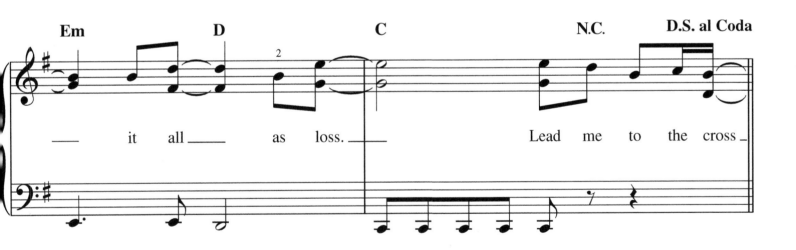

___ it all ___ as loss. ___ Lead me to the cross ___

lead me to Your heart. ___

Lead me to ___ Your heart. _____

Lead me to ___ Your heart. _____

Lead me to ___ Your heart. _____

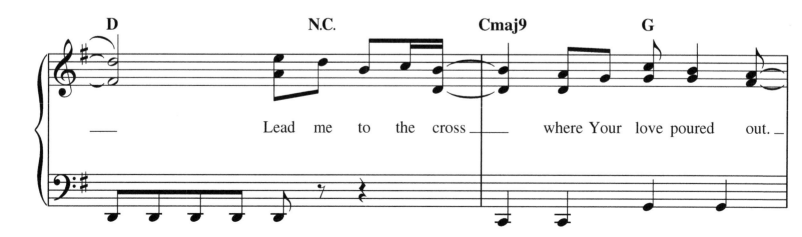

Lead me to the cross ___ where Your love poured out. __

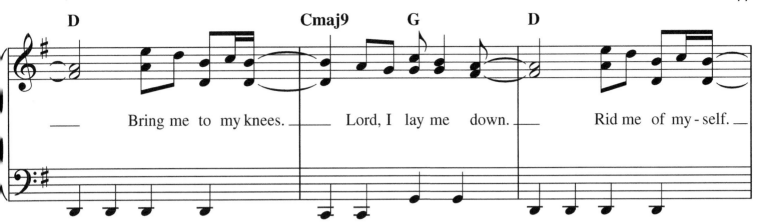

Bring me to my knees. Lord, I lay me down. Rid me of my-self.

I be-long to You. Oh, lead me,

lead me, lead me to the

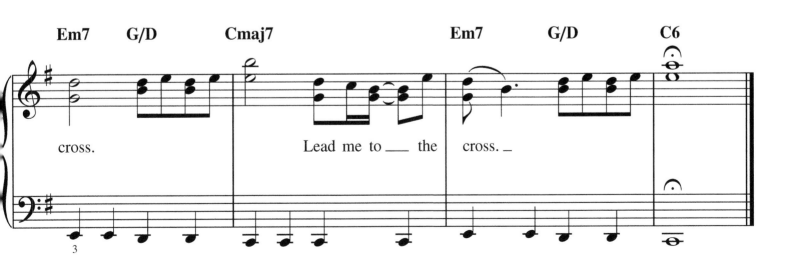

cross. Lead me to ___ the cross. ___

MADE ME GLAD

Words and Music by
MIRIAM WEBSTER

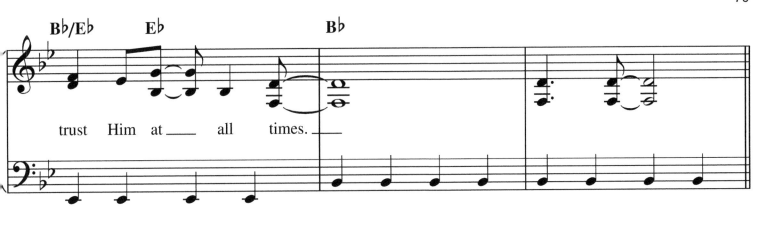

trust Him at ____ all times. ___

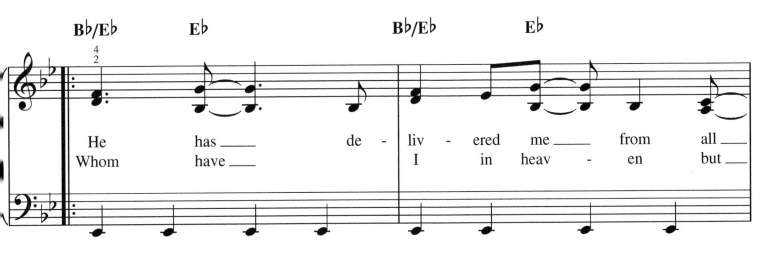

He has ____ de - liv - ered me ____ from all ____
Whom have ____ I in heav - en but ____

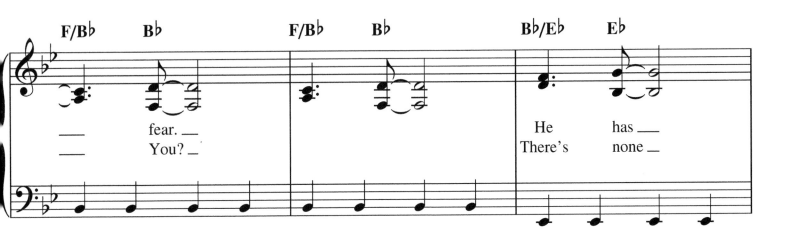

___ fear. ___
___ You? ___

He has ____
There's none ____

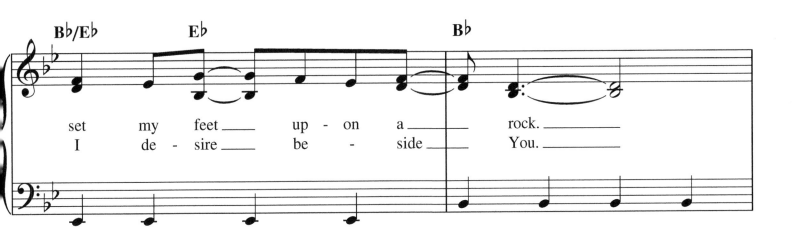

set my feet ____ up - on a ____ rock. _____
I de - sire ____ be - side ____ You. _____

I will not __ be moved, _____ and
You have made __ me glad, _____

I'll say of __ the Lord: ___ You are __ my shield, _____ my __ strength, _

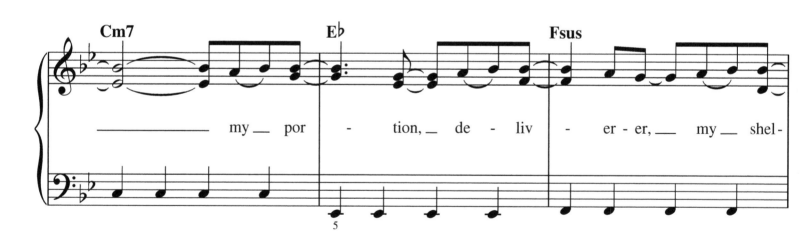

_____ my __ por - tion, __ de - liv - er - er, ___ my __ shel-

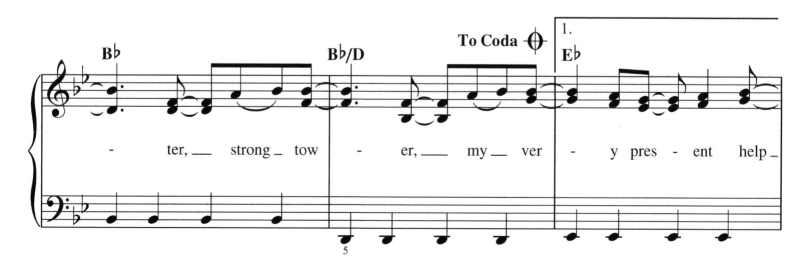

- ter, __ strong __ tow - er, ___ my __ ver - y pres - ent help __

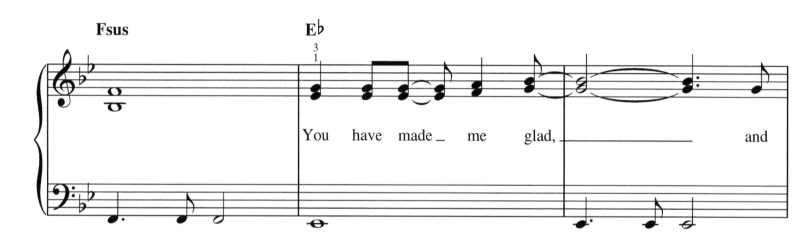

You have made ___ me glad, _____ and

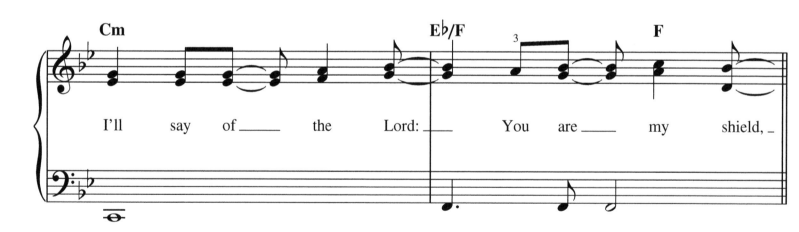

I'll say of _____ the Lord: ___ You are ___ my shield, _

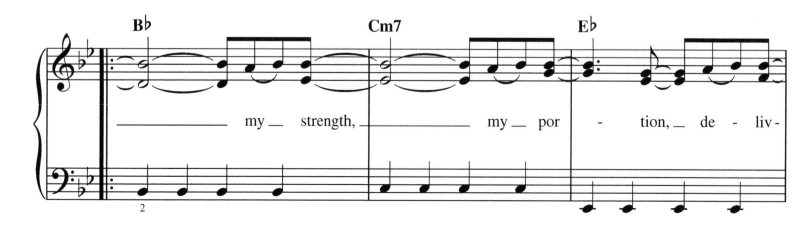

_____ my ___ strength, _____ my ___ por - tion, ___ de - liv-

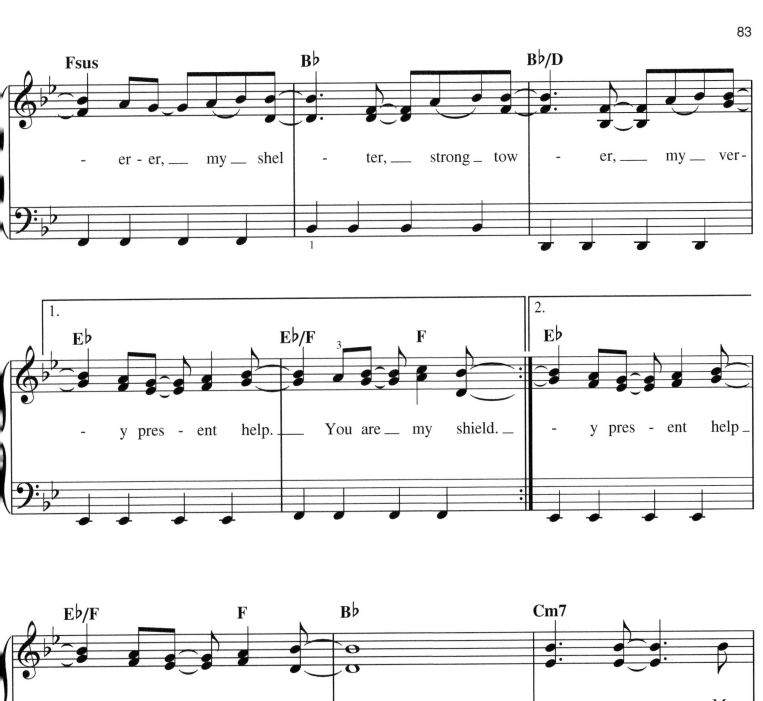

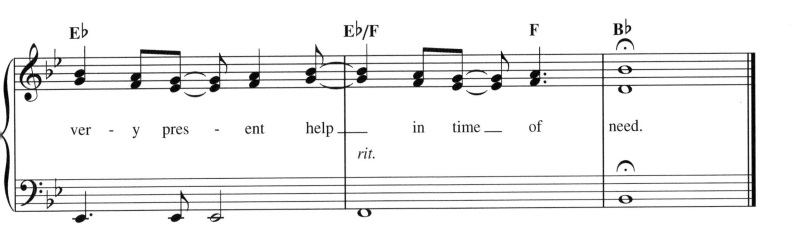

MIGHTY TO SAVE

Words and Music by BEN FIELDING
and REUBEN MORGAN

Ev-'ry-one needs com- pas-sion, a love that's nev - er
So take _ me as You find me, all my fears and

fail - ing; let mer - cy fall on me. __ Ev-'ry-one needs for -
fail - ures; fill my life a - gain. __ I give _ my life to

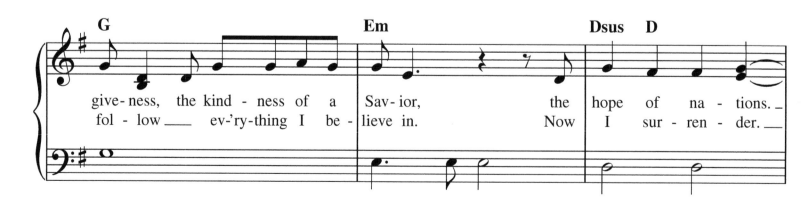

give-ness, the kind - ness of a Sav - ior, the hope of na - tions. __
fol - low _ ev'-ry-thing I be-lieve in. Now I sur - ren - der. __

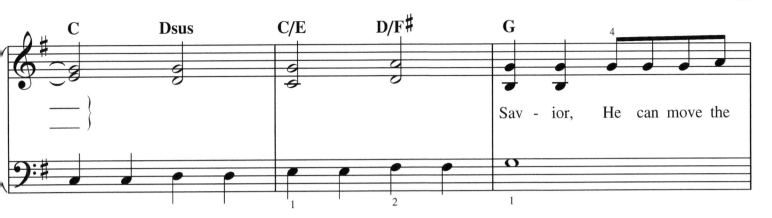

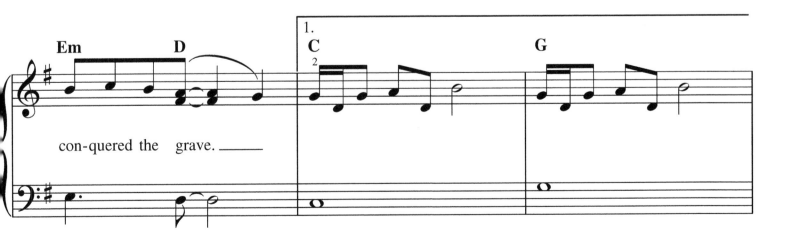

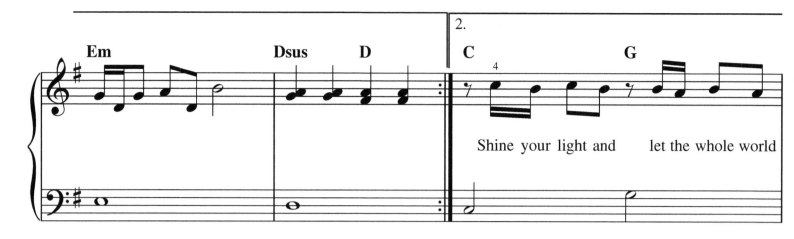

Shine your light and   let the whole world

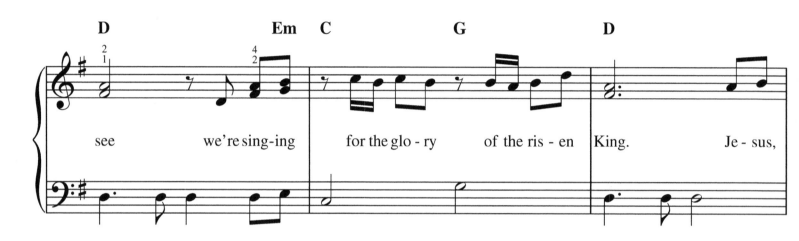

see   we're sing-ing   for the glo - ry   of the ris - en   King.   Je - sus,

shine your light and   let the whole world   see   we're sing - ing

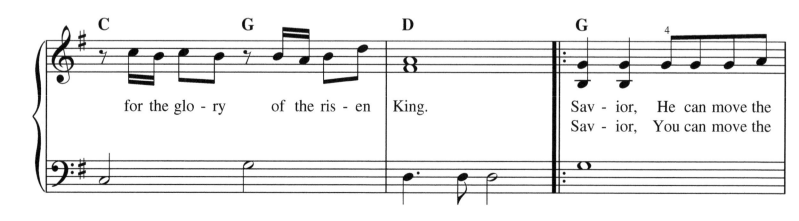

for the glo - ry   of the ris - en   King.   Sav - ior,   He can move the
Sav - ior,   You can move the

mountains. My God is mighty to save,— He is mighty to save.— For-
mountains. God, You are mighty to save,— You are mighty to save.— For-

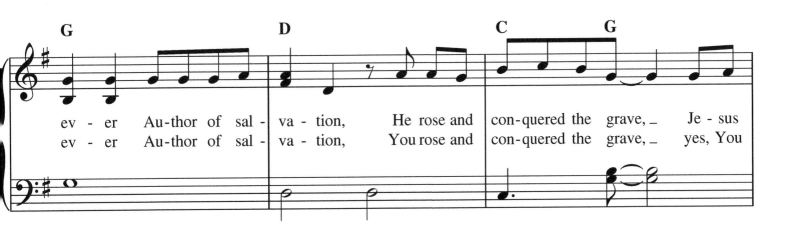

ever Author of sal- va - tion, He rose and con-quered the grave,— Je - sus
ever Author of sal- va - tion, You rose and con-quered the grave,— yes, You

1.
con-quered the grave.— You're my

2.
con-quered the grave._____

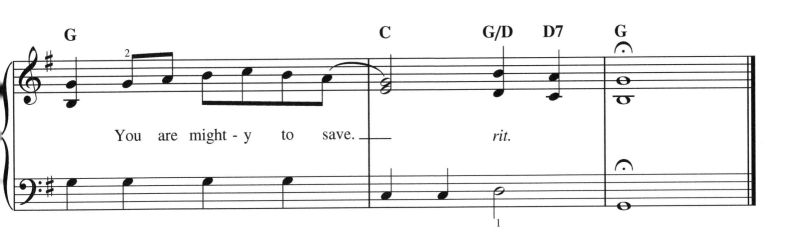

You are might-y to save._____ rit.

THE POTTER'S HAND

Words and Music by
DARLENE ZSCHECH

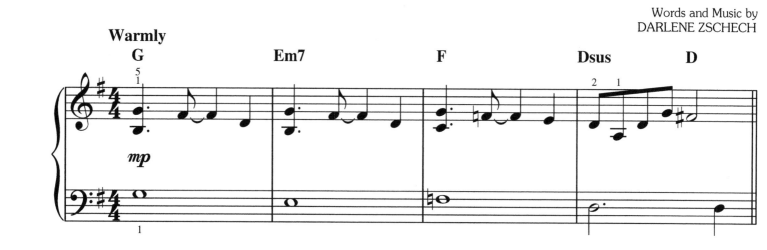

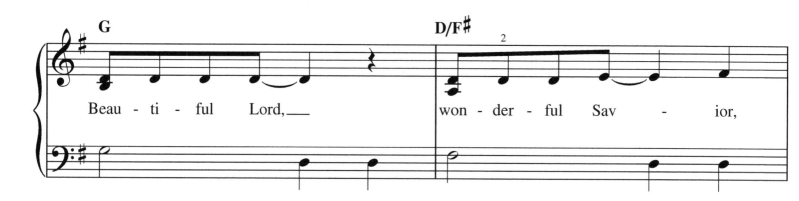

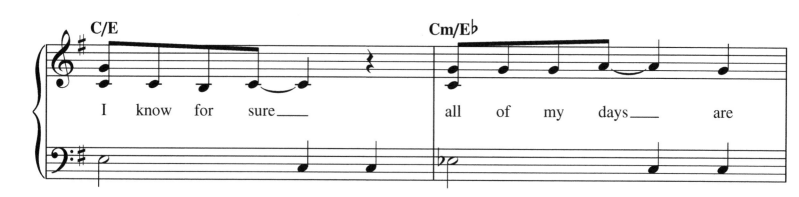

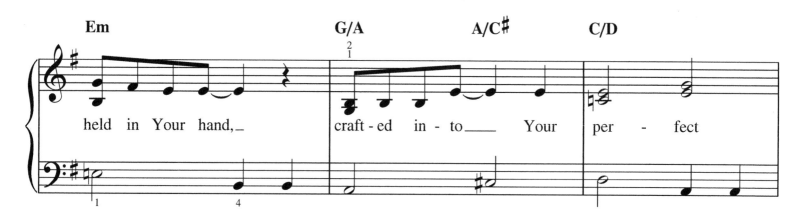

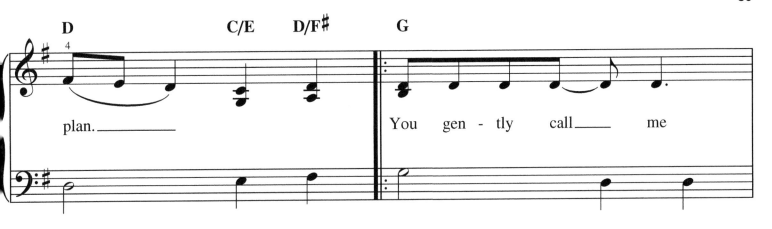

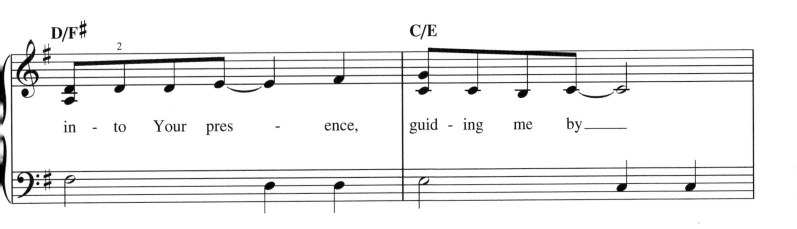

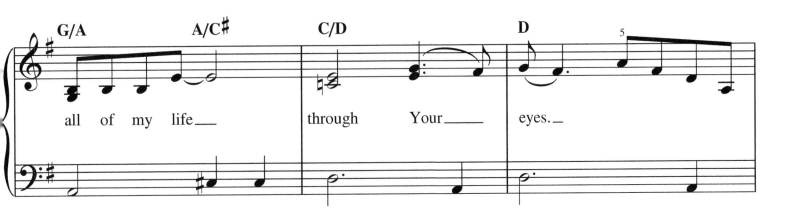

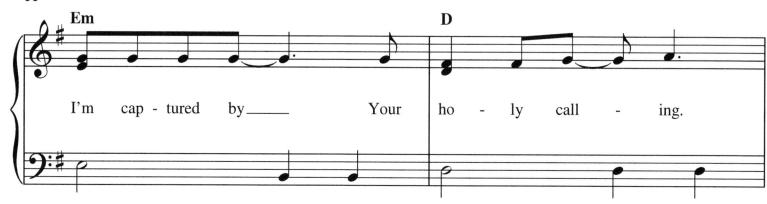

I'm cap - tured by____ Your ho - ly call - ing.

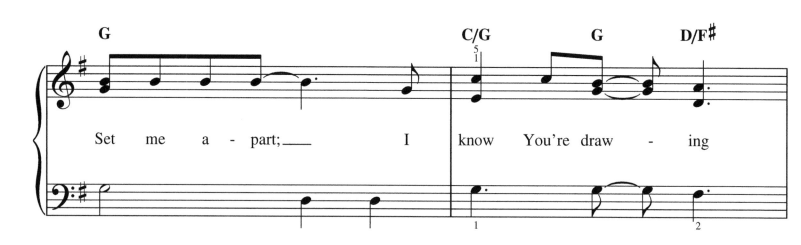

Set me a - part;____ I know You're draw - ing

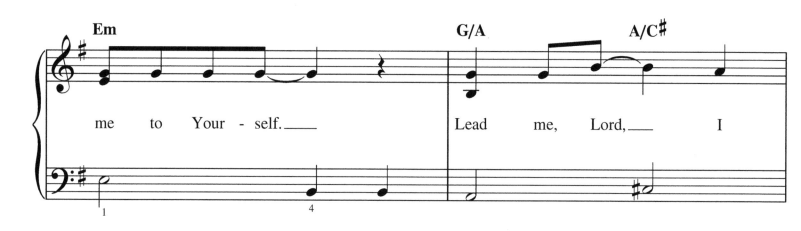

me to Your - self.____ Lead me, Lord,____ I

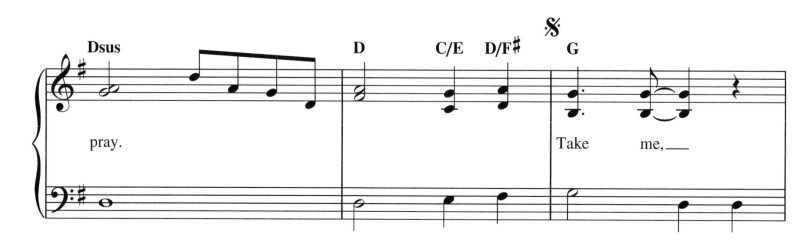

pray. Take me,____

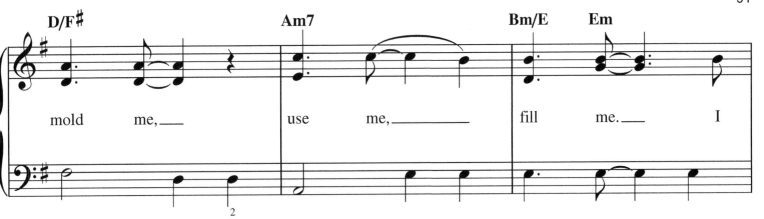

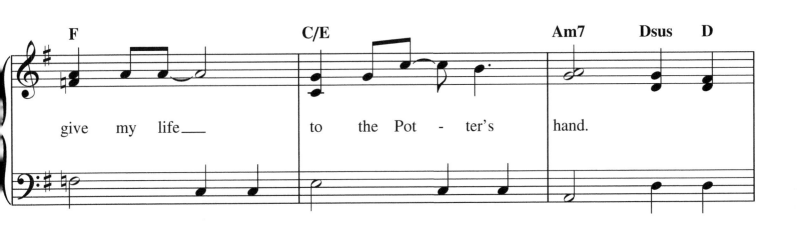

92

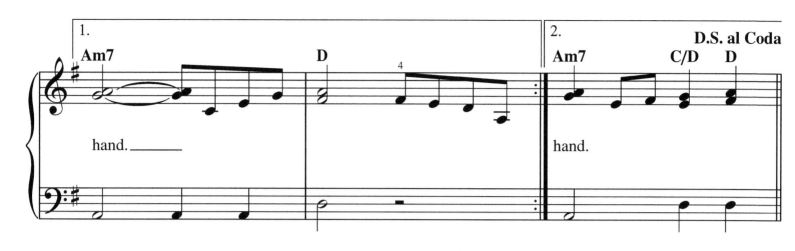

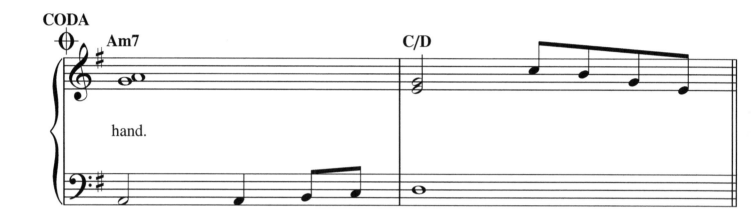

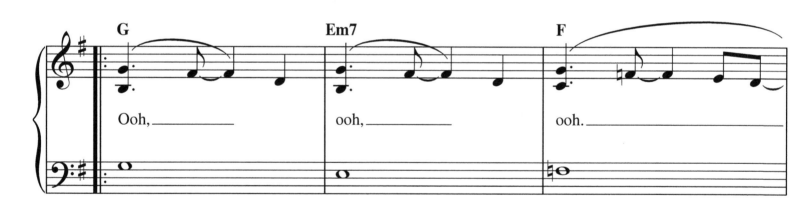

SHOUT TO THE LORD

Words and Music by
DARLENE ZSCHECH

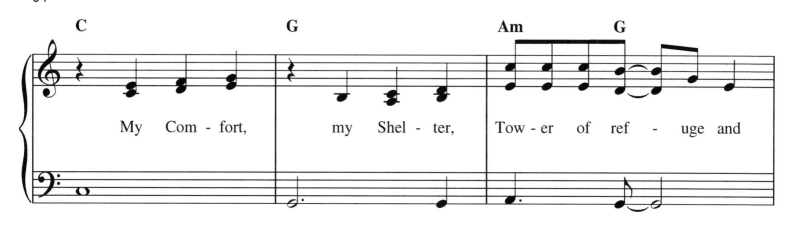

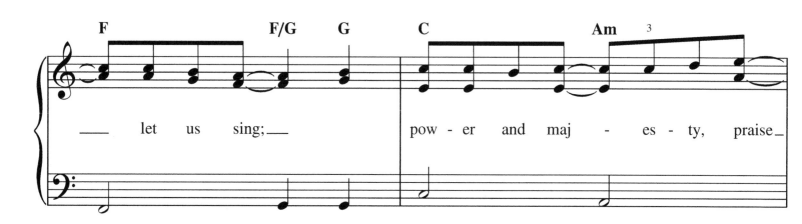

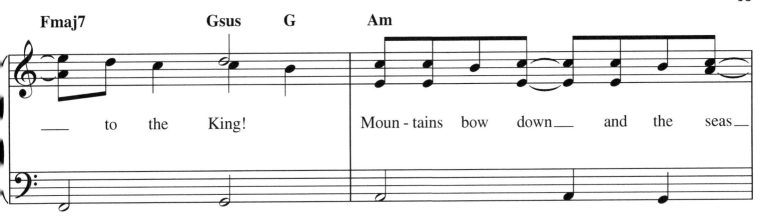

to the King! Moun-tains bow down__ and the seas__

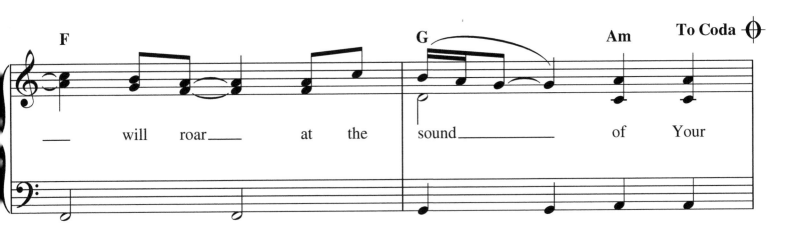

will roar__ at the sound_____ of Your

name._____ I sing for joy__ at the work__

of Your hands,__ for-ev-er I'll love__ You, for-ev-

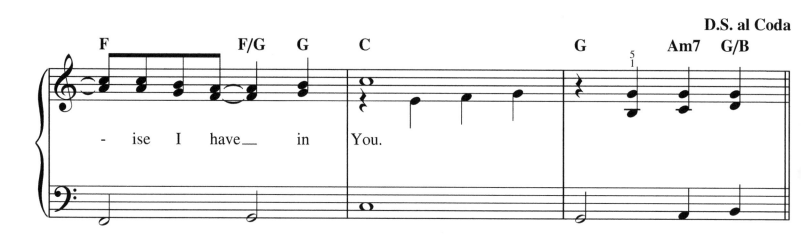

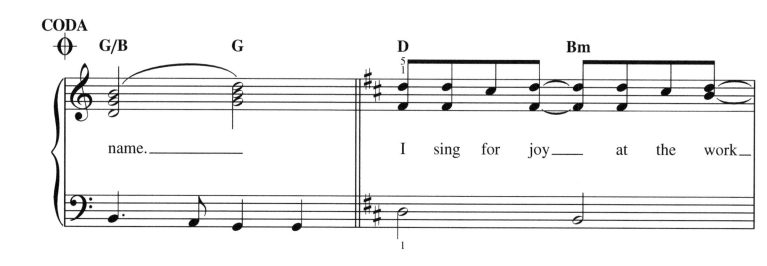

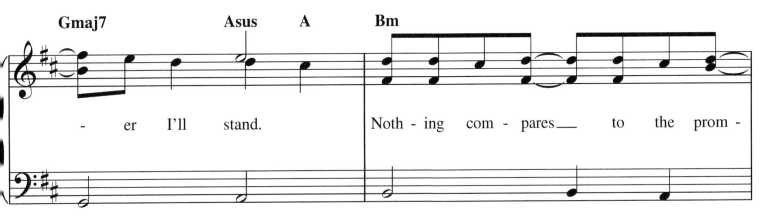

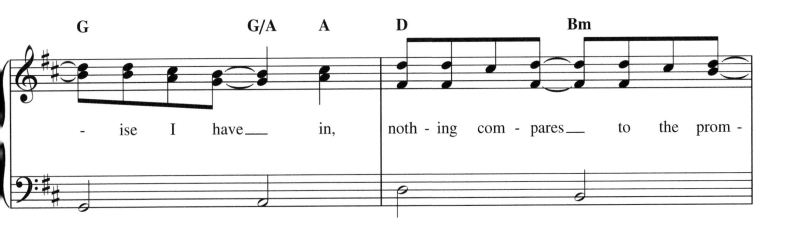

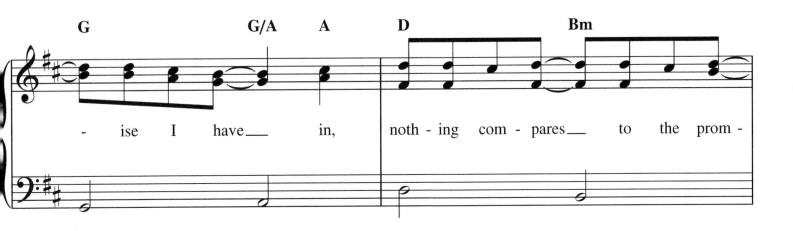

STILL

Words and Music by
REUBEN MORGAN

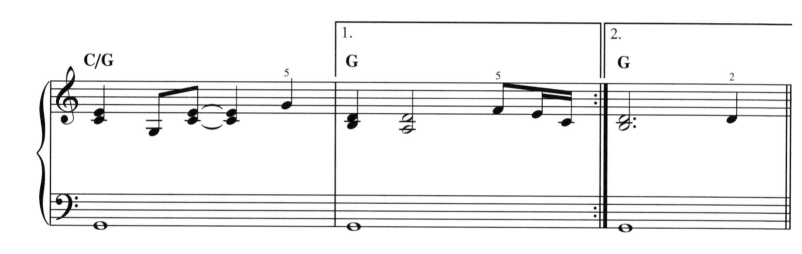

(1.) Hide me ___ now ___ un - der Your ___ wings. ___
(2.,3.) rest, my ___ soul, ___ in Christ a - lone. ___

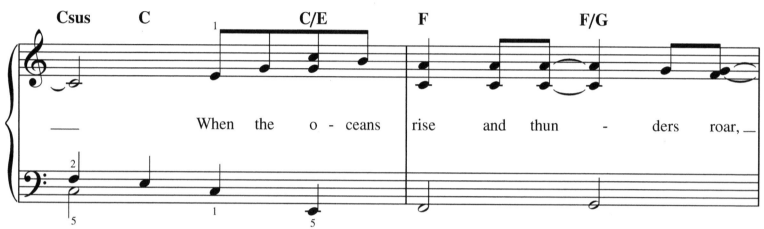

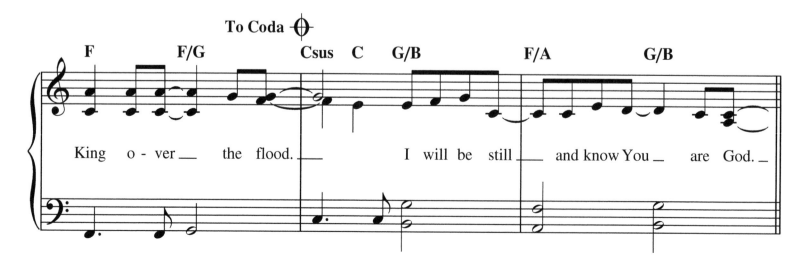

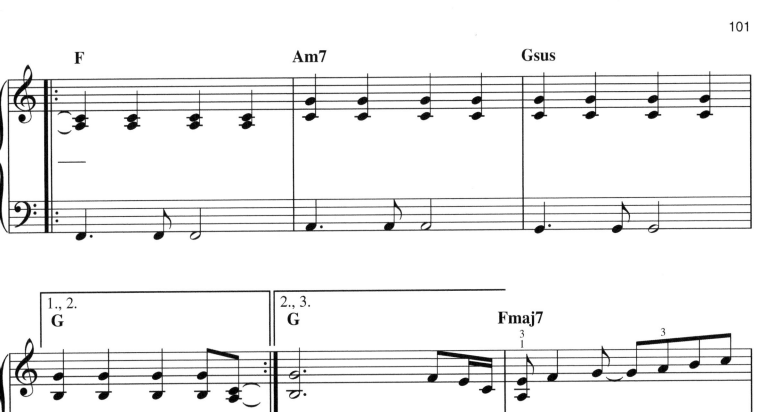

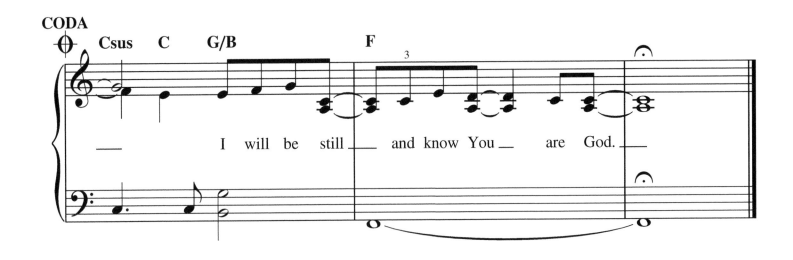

Gsus G C/E F
Cov - er me with -
Know His pow'r in
Dm Gsus C/E F F/G
in Your might - y hand. When the o-ceans rise and thun - ders roar,
qui - et - ness and trust.
Csus C C/E F G Am C/E
I will soar with You a - bove the storm. Fa - ther, You are
F F/G Csus C G/B
King o - ver the flood. I will be still and know You are God.
1.
F/A G/B

I will be still ___ and know You ___ are God. ___

STRONGER

Words and Music by BEN FIELDING
and REUBEN MORGAN

Faith - ful - me.

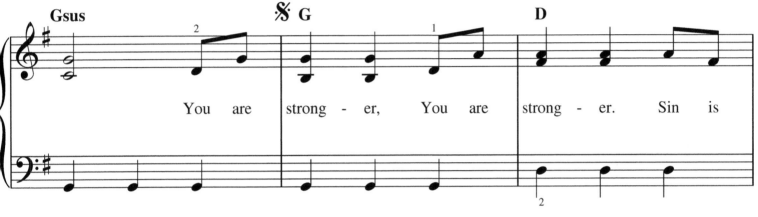

You are strong - er, You are strong - er. Sin is

bro - ken, You have saved me. It is writ - ten: Christ is

To Coda ⊕

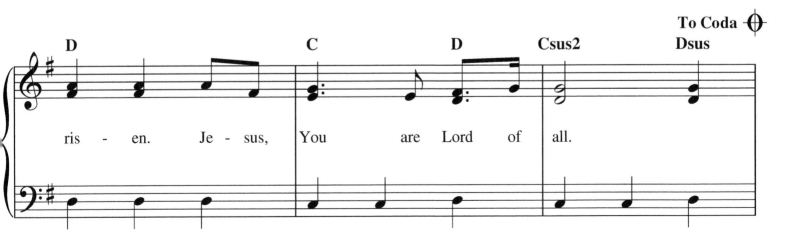

ris - en. Je - sus, You are Lord of all.

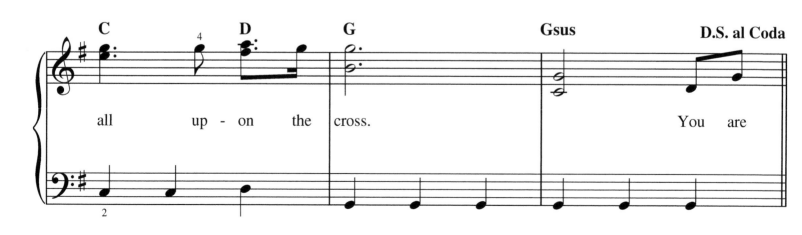

WORTHY IS THE LAMB

Words and Music by
DARLENE ZSCHECH

Worshipfully

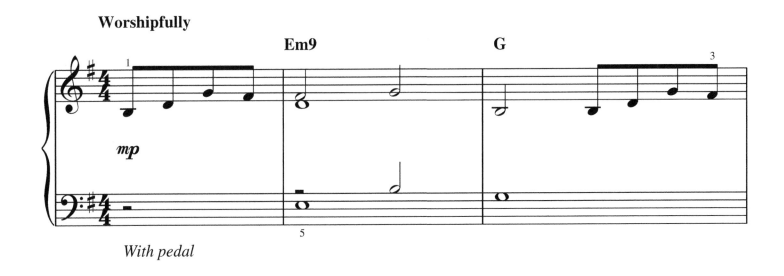

With pedal

Thank You for the cross,_____ Lord._____

Thank You for the price You paid. Bear-ing all my

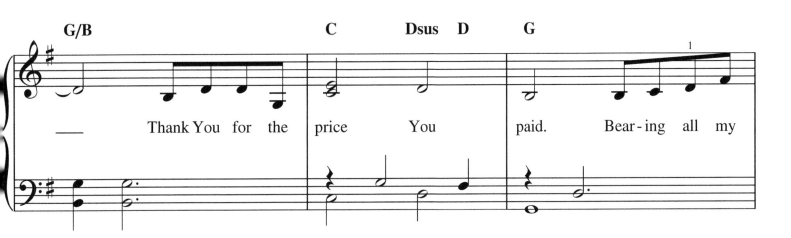

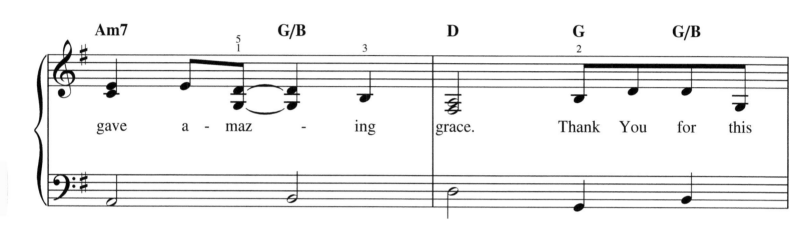

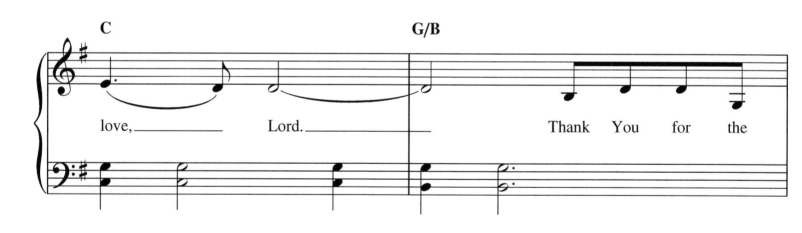

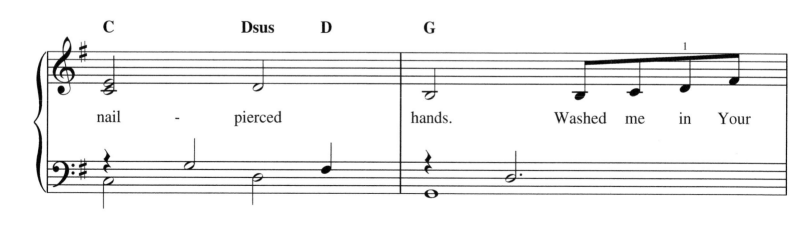

cleans - ing flow,__ now all I know,__ Your for - give - ness and__ em -

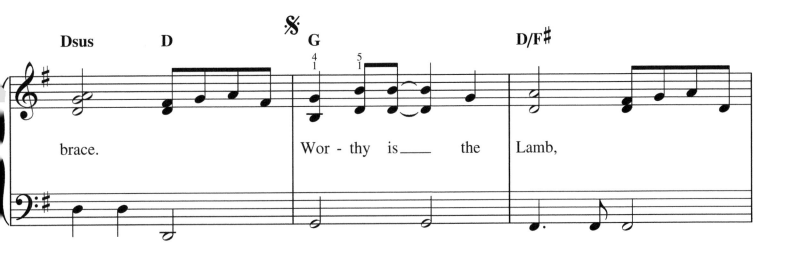

brace. Wor - thy is__ the Lamb,

seat - ed on__ the throne. Crown You now__ with

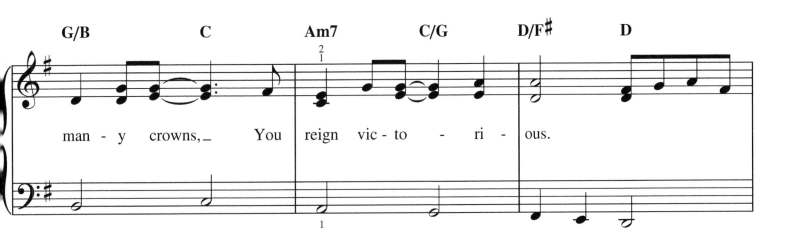

man - y crowns,__ You reign vic - to - ri - ous.

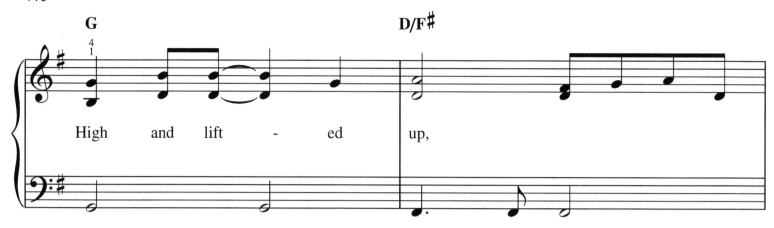

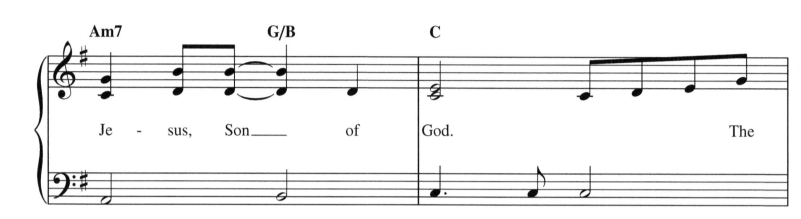

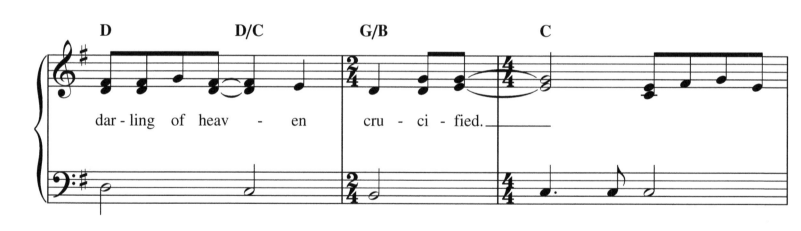

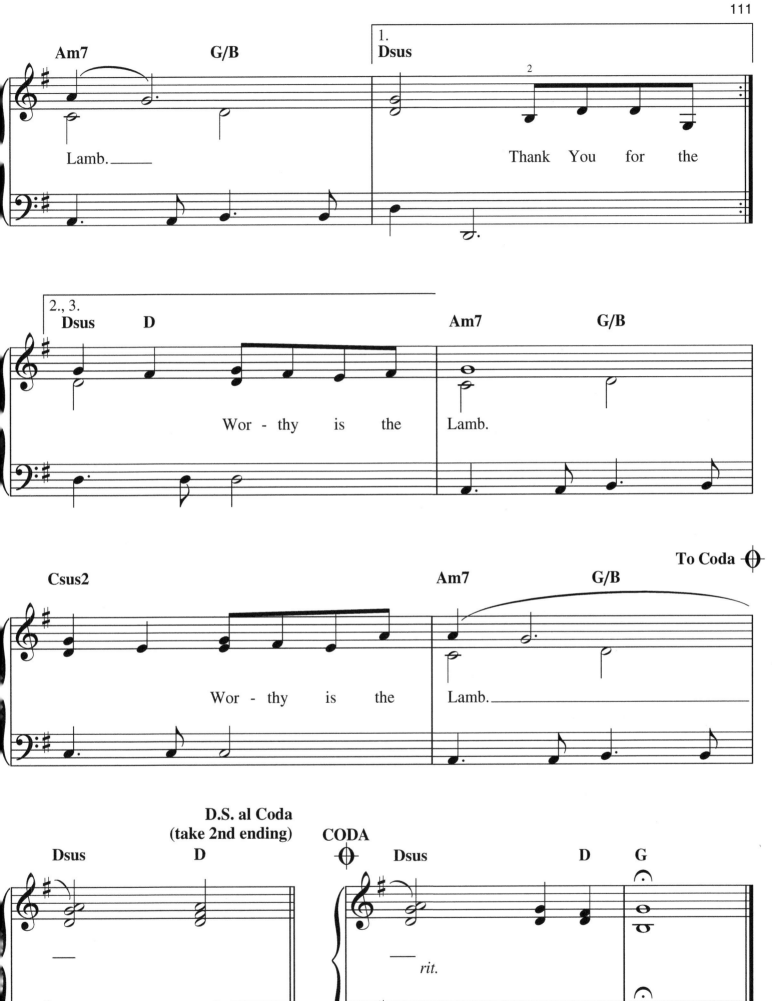